Achieving Educational Excellence for CHILDREN at RISK

Mable T. Hawkins, Editor

Selected Papers from
The NASW Third National School Social Work Conference
"Educational Excellence in Transitional Times"

January 31–February 3, 1985,
New Orleans, Louisiana

National Association of Social Workers
Silver Spring, Maryland

Cover designed by Susan B. Laufer

Cover photographs copyright © Ann Zane Shanks, *Old Is What You Get: Dialogues on Aging by the Old and the Young* (New York: Viking Press, 1976), p. 39; and copyright © Richard Balzer, *Street Time* (New York: Grossman Publishers, 1972), p. 104. Reprinted by permission of Viking Penguin Inc.

Library of Congress Cataloging-in-Publication Data

NASW National School Social Work Conference "Educational
    Excellence in Transitional Times" (3rd : 1985 : New
    Orleans, La.)
    Achieving educational excellence for children at risk.

    Includes bibliographies.
    1. School social work—United States—Congresses.
I. Hawkins, Mable T. II. Title.
LB3013.4.N38   1985   371.4'6   86-12590
ISBN 0-87101-143-3

Printed in U.S.A.

Contents

Conference Planning Committee

Mable T. Hawkins (Chair), Ph.D., is Associate Professor, School of Social Work, University of Pittsburgh, Pittsburgh, Pennsylvania. She is First Vice President of the National Association of Social Workers.

I. Lorraine Davis, MSSW, is State Supervisor, School Social Work Services, Bureau for Pupil Services, Department of Public Instruction, State of Wisconsin, Madison.

Randy A. Fisher, MSW, is School Social Worker, Mannheim District 83, Franklin Park, Illinois.

Esther K. Glasser, MSW, is a consultant in social work, Washington, D.C., and a member of the Commission on School Social Work of the National Association of Social Workers.

Betty L. Welsh, MSW, is Professor, School of Social Work, Wayne State University, Detroit, Michigan.

Introduction

Mable T. Hawkins

THREE YEARS AFTER THE publication of *A Nation at Risk*, public school improvement issues remain in the forefront of critical topics addressed by newspapers, television programs, and news magazines.[1] During this time, education has received increased attention in state legislatures and in school districts across the nation. A significant number of reports on improving schools have been published.[2] Education groups and elected officials have given serious attention to reports that were developed from special surveys conducted by various interest groups concerned with the future of our schools.[3]

The most prominent report, *A Nation at Risk*, was produced by a blue-ribbon committee appointed by former Secretary of Education, T. H. Bell. This committee, formed in August 1981 and referred to as the National Commission on Excellence in Education, was directed to examine the quality of education in the United States and to make a report to the nation within 18 months of its first meeting. The commission's report, issued in April 1983, describes why schools in the United States are mediocre and recommends specific steps for improving them, including changes in course content, merit pay for teachers whose evaluation indicates superior performance, teaching reforms, and an active citizens' role.

A significant gap in the report is an examination of needs that school children, parents, schools, and communities have in the area of human services. In view of the changing economic and sociological factors in our society, the need in the 1980s for federal education policies that address the concerns of poor, disadvantaged, handicapped, and minority students, without slighting the quality of education, is mandatory.

Responses to the commission's report from many national, regional, and state groups concerned with education were so numerous that, by February 1984, national reports on schools offered many pages of advice on how to upgrade public schools.[4] It is regrettable that these reports did not add up to a single well-developed plan for local groups to follow, but their findings confirmed that there are overlaps, contradictions, and gaps in understanding about some issues directly related to educational excellence.

The National Association of Social Workers (NASW), since its inception in 1955, has been among the leading national organizations actively engaged in advancing high-quality education for all children. In keeping with efforts to understand and promote effective educational programs, NASW sponsored its Third National School Social Work Conference, "Educational Excellence in Transitional Times," from January 31 to February 3, 1985, in New Orleans, Louisiana. The planning committee for this conference involved a broad range of professional educators, social workers, and other public school support personnel in sharing ideas for organizing and designing the conference program. The unique role of social workers in providing services to students, families, and communities, the relationship between a rapidly changing society and educational problems, and the need to develop practical approaches to the increasingly complex issues in today's schools, were major themes that were emphasized throughout the conference program.

Through a competitive process, over 300 presenters were selected to deliver papers that addressed a wide range of school-related concerns—from single parenting, school discipline, and underachievement—to child abuse, teenage parenting, and improved school-community linkages. In addition to the presenters of the diverse topics addressed during the conference, national figures in social work, education, and the U.S. Congress were also among those invited by the conference planning committee to make presentations for special institutes and plenary sessions.

A special highlight of the conference was the report of a national project conducted by the conference planning committee. In conjunction with this conference, the planning committee initiated a national study. Goals of the study were to:

> 1. Document major human, social and interpersonal factors which are barriers to achieving excellence and begin a process of dealing with these factors in order to promote excellence; and
> 2. Promote programmatic and policy changes on the national, state and local school levels to overcome these barriers and promote excellence.[5]

Findings of the study involving 500 people from 30 states were reported at the final plenary session of the conference. A description and results of the complete study have been published in a monograph entitled *The Human Factor: A Key to Excellence in Education.*[6]

It is of particular significance that the planning committee for the NASW Third National School Social Work Conference, through conducting a national survey to define excellence in education, to identify barriers to excellence in education, and to make recommendations to mitigate these barriers, has assumed a leadership position in stressing the school-environmental relationship. The fact that participants in the survey—including social workers from a range of organizations, public officials, teachers, university staff, superintendents, principals, staff of other public agencies, school boards, parents, other pupil personnel workers, and other school supervisory staff—reached general consensus on major issues lends greater validity to the study's findings.

Major human and social barriers identified by respondents to the survey reflect some of the complexities and incongruities surrounding various issues pertaining to the quality of education evident in a number of published reports on school improvement.[7] Leading barriers noted by participants in the study as interfering most with excellence in education include a cross section of family, student, school, community, and legislative issues.

Articles selected for this volume reflect the diversity of issues raised at the conference and highlight the barriers faced by children at risk in the quest for achieving educational excellence. The problems identified in these articles and the strategies for overcoming the barriers presented by these problems should be of interest both to educators and to professional practitioners who work with children in school or school-related settings. The planning committee had many difficult decisions to make in choosing the articles for the book from the wealth of material presented at the conference, and it is hoped that this selection will give the reader some flavor of the scope and substance of the entire event. The range of issues given special attention in this publication includes substance abuse, truancy, adolescent suicide, learning disabilities, desegregation, and the gifted child. Although we regret that articles on the critical issues of sexual and child abuse were not available for this book, we note the wealth of material on these topics already accessible from many other sources.

It is essential that those who are responsible for the welfare of children consider the ecological perspective in assessing barriers to excellence in education. Recognizing the potential in collaborating with community resources and using the team approach to problem-solve should enhance the effectiveness of pupil personnel staff members. Indeed, if we wish to attain high-quality education for all children, we must not fail to tap resources in the home, school, and community to assist in the achievement of our goals. Through continued sharing of our knowledge, values, and skills at conferences and seminars and through publication of our work, we may facilitate recognition of the human factor as a key to excellence in education.

In closing, I would like to acknowledge the efforts of the many individuals who invested so much of themselves in making the conference a reality and a success. The creative labor and efforts of the planning committee helped to bring the conference as well as this book to fruition. In addition to the planning committee, the following people also donated their time and energy in reviewing and selecting the numerous abstracts submitted for the conference (and some carried the additional responsibility for reviewing the pool of articles from which this volume is drawn): John Alderson, Robert Constable, Andrew V. Coughlin, Jr., Edith M. Freeman, Robert J. Gallagher, Janice Houser, E. Virginia Lapham, Fran Matthies, James G. McCullagh, Anne Mitchell, Nina F. Roby, Inta Rutins, Eleanora Thomas, and Sheila Young. I am also grateful to all those staff members of NASW who worked so hard both before and during the conference to ensure its success—and particularly to Isadora Hare, Sheldon R. Goldstein, Georgianna Carrington, and Marlis McCollum—and to the NASW editorial staff for their efforts and help in developing and producing this volume. Not least do I wish to express my sincere appreciation to all those who prepared and presented papers at the conference, for without their outstanding contributions, there would indeed have been no conference at all.

Notes and References

1. National Commission on Excellence in Education, U.S. Department of Education, *A Nation at Risk: The Imperative for Educational Reform* (Washington, D.C.: U.S. Government Printing Office, 1983).

2. See, for example, B. Rodman, "Carnegie's Panel on Teaching Will Urge Major Restructuring of Nation's Schools," *Education Week: American Education's Newspaper of Record* (Washington, D.C.), 5, No. 30 (April 16, 1986), pp. 1, 42; and D. Davies, "A Nation at Risk—An Opportunity for School Reform," *Citizen Action in Education and Resources for Youth* (Boston: Institute for Responsive Education and National Commission on Resources for Youth, 1983).

3. E. Bowen, "Way, Way Back to Basics," *Time*, December 2, 1985; J. Murphy et al., "School Effectiveness: A Conceptual Framework," *Educational Forum*, 49 (Spring 1985); and E. M. Freeman, "Analyzing the Organizational Content of Schools," *Social Work in Education*, 7 (Spring 1985), pp. 141-159.

4. Massachusetts Advocacy Center, *Our Children at Risk: The Crisis in Public Education* (Boston: Massachusetts Advocacy Center, 1984); R. Zerchykov, "The Middle Grades Assessment Program in Action," *Citizen Action in Education*, 10, No. 2 (1984); and J. R. Berrueta-Clement et al., *Changed Lives: The Effect of the Perry Preschool Program on Youths through Age 19* (Ypsilanti, Mich.: High/Scope Press, 1984).

5. P. Mintzies and I. Hare, *The Human Factor: A Key to Excellence in Education* (Silver Spring, Md.: National Association of Social Workers, 1985), p. 7.

6. Ibid.

7. J. I. Goodlad, *A Place Called School: Prospects for the Future* (New York: McGraw-Hill Book Co., 1984); S. R. Rose, "Development of Children's Social Competence in Classroom Groups," *Social Work in Education*, 8 (Fall 1985), pp. 48-58; and J. A. Hatch, "Technology and the Devaluation of Human Processes," *Educational Forum*, 48, No. 2 (1984).

Group Work with Gifted Children: A School Resource

Jackolyn W. Durrett
Susan H. Dawson
Mary Constance Patterson
Valerie Gray

THE PURPOSE OF THIS ARTICLE is to discuss techniques for identification of and intervention with underachieving gifted children in a rural junior high school setting. Analysis of this project illustrates that social workers are in a unique position to address the dynamics of school-family-child interactions concerning underachieving gifted children. The project demonstrates that social workers can meet effectively the special needs of gifted students.

Two percent of the school population—2.5 million students—are gifted.[1] Gifted students are at high risk in American school systems. The following statistics may serve to verify this designation:

- 65 percent of the gifted are unidentified[2]

- 57.5 percent of school administrators indicate they have *no* gifted students in their school[3]

- 30 percent of high school dropouts have intelligence quotients over 135[4]

- 50 percent of gifted students are performing two to four grades below ability[5]

- 11 percent of gifted males and 10 percent of gifted females do not finish high school[6]

• Fewer than 50 percent of gifted students are referred for testing by teachers.[7]

The foregoing data indicate gifted students are at risk of being unidentified at school and of underachieving. Other data indicated that giftedness contributes to behavioral problems such children experience at school.[8] As a consequence, social workers see gifted children, not recognized as gifted, who are referred for behavioral or emotional problems and may be labeled as behavior disordered, learning disabled, or emotionally disturbed. This suggests that essential competencies of school social workers should include the ability to identify gifted children and to assess the particular patterns of gifted students' functioning that contribute to behavioral and emotional problems.

The Identification Process

Some characteristics of gifted children that aid in the identification process include: emotional sensitivity, divergent thinking, extreme self-criticism, high energy levels, a tendency to fantasize or daydream, intensity, persistence, incessant questioning, and humor. When these characteristics are internalized by the child as positive paths to personal growth and integrity, the result is a developmentally healthy and academically achieving student who is generally recognized as a gifted individual. However, some of these same characteristics, when improperly channeled, can create such intensely adverse conditions for the gifted child that he or she is not only an underachiever but also quite possibly unidentified as a gifted child.

In a study of highly gifted underachieving children at the primary level, Whitmore found a number of positive traits that were associated with specific difficulties in a majority of children.[9] These included: acute perceptiveness and emotional sensitivity, which were frequently displayed or perceived as hyperactivity and/or distractibility; an independent nature, exhibited through disruptive behavior and a questioning of authority and rules; initiative, which created problems in the child's willingness to accept societal or environmental constraints; an exploring nature, often perceived as stubbornness and a tendency to stray from a task; and a distinct learning style, which interfered with the child's responsiveness to traditional teaching methods such as drill exercises, thus causing the child to be perceived as lazy or unmotivated.

Fine and Pitts reported that gifted children often present an interpersonal attitude that fosters social isolation and may contribute to poor teacher-student relationships.[10] This attitude consists of an "I'm ok—you're not ok" position that uses ridicule and sarcasm to establish superiority. Other studies have found that under-achieving gifted children often display hostility toward authoritarian figures, select peers who reinforce negative attitudes toward school, and exhibit marked withdrawal in the classroom.[11]

Teacher assessments and academic records of the students in our study support previous findings. We were able to document instances of several of the aforementioned characteristics in all group members and also, in one case, to observe intense dislike toward a particular student resulting from his "I'm ok—you're not ok" attitude.

School Adjustment of the Gifted Child

In addition to the gifted child's characteristics, there are school structures and other environmental factors that tend to complicate the school adjustment of the gifted student. Five examples are

- Rejection of the gifted child's nonconformity or achievement

- Unrealistic expectation of teachers, parents, and self

- School curriculum geared for the average student

- Teaching and instructional style of most teachers

- Classroom climate emphasizing competition, recognition of differences, and utilization of group interaction.[12]

Gifted children often experience peer or teacher rejection because of their resistance to conforming to expected rules and their questioning or challenging of authority. American society values innovation and difference but tends to reward conformity. Often other students and sometimes even teachers are consciously or unconsciously jealous of the gifted student's intellectual ability. This can lead to a gifted student who reveals exceptional ability being isolated; therefore, some gifted students hide their ability to maintain social acceptance.

If a child is identified as gifted, teachers or parents often have unrealistic expectations for the child because they are not aware that intellectual giftedness is not generalized to emotional or physical maturity. The gifted might have the knowledge of an adult but react emotionally in an immature, childish fashion. In addition, teachers and parents often receive gratification from a gifted student's achievement and unconsciously or actively pressure the student for further achievement. However, the most difficult expectation to deal with is the tendency of the gifted student to expect perfection of self and hence to set unrealistic goals.

The curriculum of the normal classroom is geared to the average student, who primarily uses convergent thinking patterns. The gifted student tends to use divergent thinking patterns and resist acceptance of facts and information without lengthy explanation, mental effort, and time to assimilate knowledge through association.

Gifted students often come to elementary school knowing much of what is taught in the first three grades. The students' internal push to know and understand is lowered when what is being presented is already known to them. Webb, Meckstroth, and Tolan stated that gifted elementary school students have one quarter or one half their time left over when they have completed their work.[13] Exceptionally gifted students may have three quarters of their class time with little to do. Hence they become disruptive, daydream, or try to entertain themselves.

The average classroom teacher assumes the role of expert imparter of knowledge and expects the student to be a passive recipient. Gifted students thrive in circumstances where they can assimilate knowledge through association rather than through concrete presentation followed by rote drills. The gifted student thus tends to resist, openly question, or even openly rebel against traditional instructional methods.

The social tendency of gifted students to manipulate, be aggressive, or withdraw from peer interaction presents problems in the classroom. But there are three other classroom conditions that can complicate peer interaction.[14] These are the extent to which individual differences are truly valued, the degree of competition that is fostered, and the type and amount of peer interaction. Gifted students are different, and they need a classroom atmosphere that accepts or at least tolerates uniqueness. The amount and kind of competition that is fostered is critical to the gifted students' adjustment since competition may increase rejection or jealousy by fellow students. Also, the combination of the self-expectation for perfection and a competitive classroom climate makes for an unmanageable level of anxiety in many gifted students.

It is clear that gifted students' adjustment to the school environment and their attainment of their full potential is complicated by the interaction of their personality and the structure of the regular classroom. With this understanding, social workers can assist teachers, parents, and school officials to work with the gifted students toward positive adjustment. One intervention strategy that has proved successful with the gifted and gifted underachievers is social skills training groups; peer-group activity provides opportunity to learn the give and take of social situations.[15]

Social Skills Training with Gifted Nonachievers

Social skills training was chosen as an intervention strategy with four underachieving gifted early adolescents at a nonurban school in Louisiana. A routine third-year reevaluation using teacher assessment and student record review revealed that these males were exhibiting marked withdrawal within the classroom; superior attitudes toward peers and school personnel; academic failure or lack of achievement; independent nature, displayed through active questioning of rules and resulting disciplinary infractions; and, in all cases, a strong resistance to traditional teaching methods, including a refusal to perform rote drill and homework.

As a result of these behavior patterns, these students were perceived overwhelmingly by their teachers as being unmotivated, posing difficult behavior problems in the classroom, and being socially dysfunctional in peer interactions. These assessment characteristics identified in the group members support the previous findings of Clark and of Fine and Pitts.[16] A social skills training group was structured as a means to reach the following goals or outcomes with these students:

- Improve behavior in the regular classroom
- Increase attendance
- Foster positive peer interaction
- Decrease disciplinary actions
- Improve academic achievement.

It was thought that a social skills training group could have some of these effects because it met the needs of all adolescents to become proficient in social skills as well as some of the unique needs of underachieving gifted students.

Manaster, in his book *Adolescent Development and Life Tasks*, described a variety of skills that all adolescents must master.[17] Some of these skills are needed in the school environment as well as in the adult world. Many of these skills are particularly relevant to gifted nonachievers placed in a regular classroom with very limited, if any, individual instruction. These crucial skills are

- Dealing with lover, sex, peer relationships
- Coordinating actions with peers
- Managing stress and frustration
- Coping with one's own aggression and that of others
- Dealing with feelings
- Dealing with group pressure
- Dealing with authority figures
- Being able to negotiate conflicts
- Planning
- Exhibiting self-control

The following description of this social skills program covers structure, strategies, and techniques. The social skills program consisted of thirteen sessions, each of thirty minutes duration, with four underachieving male students in a rural middle school. The sessions were designed around topics focused on the intellectual, personal, and environmental needs of these gifted underachieving students. The social skills group sessions included the following:

Duration	Content
One session	Group purpose, goals, topics, methods, techniques, housekeeping items, checklist completion
One session	Values clarification exercise and discussion of values relative to communication
Six sessions	Feelings

Duration	Content
Two sessions	Body language
One session	Assertive vs. aggressive responses and behavior
One session	Integration of the above topics
One session	Termination and group party

The first session was dedicated to a statement of the group's purpose, goals, methods, topics, and techniques to be used in the attainment of the purposes and goals. Major activities planned were role-playing, modeling of appropriate behaviors and responses, discussion of personal experiences, and experiential exercises. Housekeeping items were taken care of; rules were established governing confidentiality and situations in which the facilitator would intervene. After this discussion, the students filled out Goldstein et al.'s social skills checklist.[18] Completion of the checklist provided each student with an assessment of his strong and weak areas in social skills. Parents and teachers also completed an identical checklist during the first week of the program. This was added to other baseline data: current grades, achievement scores, and attendance and disciplinary reports available from school sources.

The second session focused on a discussion of the social skills checklists as well as the completion of a values clarification exercise, with further discussion centered on ways in which sound social skills and personal values affect both verbal and nonverbal interactions and communication. This appealed to the students' individuality and positive acceptance of others' views and stances.

Six sessions were devoted to the recognition and expression of feelings with specific emphasis placed on discussions of anger and its management, frustration management, boredom, and stress reduction methods that could be used at school or at home.

Two sessions centered on body language and one on assertive versus aggressive responses and behaviors. Another session briefly integrated all topics discussed by the group and terminated with the participants' evaluation of the group experience as well as completion of the posttest checklist. Again, parents and teachers also completed identical checklists. The last session focused on termination and a group party.

The strategies and techniques used with this group were as important as the content presented in meeting the members' unique needs. A safe but controlled environment was established for group participants at the first session. The members were told that the group was to be a place where they were free to ventilate their feelings about parents, siblings, teachers, school administrators, and peers without fear of authoritarian recrimination. This left the door open for them to interact with an adult, person-to-person. As noted, these young men were having difficulty in their encounters with parents, teachers, the principal, and the assistant principal.

For the most part, members of the group had been socially ostracized in one way or another by adults and their peers. They were, as a result, experiencing social isolation, regression, and withdrawal from social interaction. Some avoided peer contact on the playground and the lunchroom and most offered little or no eye contact. Their communication through words and body language tended to be either apathetic or aggressive. Parents confirmed that these deficit communication problems extended across students' environments so that many were not school-specific. Indeed, even their preferred pastimes reflected their preference for solitary activity: reading a book, walking alone, playing alone with a computer. Isolation from peers was also encouraged by the geographic distance from neighbors inherent in a rural setting. The group experience, therefore, offered these students the opportunity to interact and share with peers who were experiencing similar frustration and isolation.

The majority of participants had begun aggressive or passive-aggressive acting out as a result of their need for some special attention even if that attention was negative, so that discipline at school had become a serious problem for them. This type of acting-out behavior was evident in the first few group sessions in the form of one member constantly interrupting whoever was speaking, another staring out of the window, and another refusing to participate in any way.

These students had become unable to develop and maintain satisfying interpersonal relationships with their teachers to the point that they would not contribute within the classroom to the instructional process or even raise their hands in class to ask for clarification. In an effort to counteract this behavioral pattern, the facilitator purposely used complex and foreign terms in group discussions and stated that the students were to stop her whenever she used a term they did not understand. Some terms used were "functional and dysfunctional interactions," "perceptions," and "precipitating events." The group members gradually became more comfortable with stopping the facilitator for clarification; then they themselves began to incorporate such terms into the discussions. A strategy used to address the group members' supersensitivity (so characteristic of gifted youngsters) was to hold group sessions in a classroom that was physically separate from the main building, thus providing an environment that was quieter and freer from sensory distractions than other available classrooms.

Group consensus that criticism would be of a constructive nature only and that confidentiality would be respected throughout the duration of the group aided in building an emotionally secure atmosphere for members. Never, at any time, was the facilitator forced to intervene in the group process in order to stop destructive criticism. Contacts with parents confirmed that the students were, indeed, taking the rule of confidentiality seriously. Group members had been told that they were free to discuss with their parents whatever they felt comfortable sharing about the group as long as they focused on their own participation and did not violate the confidentiality of any other group member. Several parents were experiencing frustration at the fact that their sons would not discuss the group with them at all. This point of confidentiality was one area around which the group formed a bond and began to develop cohesiveness.

Divergent thinking was encouraged within the group sessions. Very often, to an outside observer, it would have appeared that the group was off-task when, in reality, it was very much on-task. For example, during a session on body language, the group discussed lemmings, beached whales, bees, and Ameslan research with primates in addition to mimes and the deaf. Their high-level associative processes were able to integrate seemingly unrelated concepts. Often, the divergent thinking of one group member acted as a catalyst for the others so that group sessions offered these students a school-based rest and relaxation, if you will, from the pressures of conformity evident within the classroom environment.

The expression of feelings was difficult for these young men. Most of them had reached a point where their feelings were either being repressed or contained or were being expressed in open aggression. In any case, they were receiving few positive "strokes" or support for vocal expression of feelings. The strategy used in this regard was to present the group with hypothetical situations and to have them express their feelings relative to those situations, such as typical family or student-teacher conflicts. These exercises were relatively safe for group members in that they were removed from their own life experiences, thus making their expressed feelings conjecture rather than reality. Gradually, however, member by member, they began to offer personal feelings and situations for discussion. At this point, even negative feelings were accepted and the honesty of expression rewarded through verbal praise. Perhaps because of their tendency toward perfectionism, it was difficult for two members, in particular, to accept praise of any sort. They would react to it by lowering their heads, breaking off eye contact, or not acknowledging it verbally at all. By the seventh session, however, members began congratulating each other on school accomplishments that had come to their attention: One member had given an excellent social studies presentation in class; another member had made the football team for the coming year; and a third member had won a ribbon for a class project.

The lack of satisfying peer interaction on the part of all group members was validated by the group members themselves, teachers, parents, the principal, and the assistant principals. Indeed, during the first group meeting, all members were noticeably uncomfortable even introducing themselves to each other. For the first three sessions, all verbal interaction took place between the facilitator and individual group members with only cursory interaction among the members themselves. From the fourth session onward, the facilitator began throwing members' questions back to the group with the result that the group began assisting each other in problem solving.

Modeling and role-playing were the most effective strategies for teaching social skills to the group. They were particularly helpful techniques in lessening participants' resistance to trying new behaviors. Some of the behaviors modeled and role-played were these: how to start a conversation during recess, how to ask for clarification in class, and how to demonstrate consistency between words and actions.

Outcomes

Four reference points were used to measure outcomes of the program: grade point average, school attendance, number and severity of disciplinary referrals, and the social skills checklist. Comparison of data collected before and after group work showed that the group members improved in all four areas: grades, attendance, classroom behavior, and identified social skills.

The most notable outcomes were the improvements in social functioning indicated by the social skills checklist, which was administered to each group member, his parents, and his teachers before the group began and after the group terminated. The areas in which improvement was noted by teachers were beginning social skills, advanced social skills, skills for dealing with stress, and skills for dealing with feelings. Parents recorded gains in two of the same areas: advanced social skills and skills for dealing with stress. The student checklist scores reflected gains in beginning social skills and skills for alternatives to aggression.

The grade point average for the group overall rose from 2.78 to 3.16. The student who joined the group in progress gained .06 in his grade point average. One student improved his reading grade from an F to a B, and another student who had been making an F in mathematics made an A after group work.

Group members attended school more regularly. During a comparable period of time immediately prior to group work, they had twenty-one absences, whereas there were only six in a similar time period during group work.

Referrals for disciplinary infractions continued; however, the school principal and assistant principal voluntarily reported that the nature of the classroom misbehaviors leading to disciplinary referrals was much less serious than before the group work.

An analysis of data indicated that the group work was effective in raising the level of functioning of each member in both social and academic areas. Seven months later, group members were observed to be maintaining or improving upon their gains. The project has been expanded to other Louisiana school systems.

Implications

An analysis of this project suggests three major implications. Giftedness is a high-risk exceptionality; gifted children have special needs that school social workers can meet effectively. In order to facilitate optimal service delivery to the gifted students who present problems, social workers have the responsibility to be active in identification, planning, service delivery, and systematic evaluation of services for these children. When school social workers implement a comprehensive range of services for underachieving gifted students, the outcomes can be preventive as well as rehabilitative. These implications will now be elaborated.

Since only an approximate 2 percent of the school population meet the criteria of giftedness, it can be said that giftedness is, indeed, an exceptionality. A review of the literature on gifted children illuminates the idea that the academic and social needs of these children are associated with their giftedness. Contrary to the popular belief that the intellectually well endowed are well adjusted, statistics from a variety of studies indicate that gifted children are vulnerable to experiencing academic underachievement and maladaptive social relations. School social workers can help gifted children who have these problems. In some school systems, a pilot project can demonstrate how social workers are effective. Such a demonstration may be necessary for educators' full acceptance of the special needs of gifted students and the need for school social services for this population.

An examination of this project shows that social workers share responsibilities in a broad range of services for gifted students. The first activity is to aid teachers and school administrators in recognizing which students are gifted. Intelligence tests, grade placement measures, and interim report cards are some of the school records that can be used to confirm observational and interview data from children's parents and teachers. Research findings point out that parents are the most reliable identifiers of giftedness and that teachers are much less likely to recognize which of their pupils are gifted; therefore, social workers have a responsibility to consider giftedness as a possible explanation for certain academic and classroom behavior problems. Social workers must encourage school personnel to have such children assessed and classified within this exceptionality.

The second activity is to identify gifted children who are underachieving or manifesting symptoms of other school adjustment problems. This can be accomplished through a comparison of the students' appraised potential with their recorded academic performance. Gifted children with social skills deficits also can be identified by a systematic review of disciplinary referrals, followed by observations of their school behavior and collaborative teacher conferences. After identifying those gifted students needing services, social workers can plan an individual or group approach to alleviate their specific problems and then proceed with implementation and evaluation, being careful to include the children, their parents, and school personnel in each phase of intervention.

Systematic periodic review of the social and academic functioning levels of gifted students can promote early detection of underachievement and incipient deficits in social skills, thus enabling social workers to accomplish preventive as well as rehabilitative intervention. This kind of systematic approach can be undertaken convincingly when school social workers demonstrate effectiveness and are active in all phases of school support and related services.

Notes and References

1. J. T. Webb, E. Meckstroth, and S. Tolan, *Guiding the Gifted Child* (Columbus: Ohio Psychology Publishing Co., 1982).

2. Ibid.

3. Ibid.

4. P. Lemov, "That Kid Is Smart," *The Washingtonian*, 15, No. 3 (1979), pp. 225–233.

5. V. Gray, "An Analysis of the Effectiveness of a Parental Workshop: Increasing Parental Strengths in Rearing Preschool Gifted Children." Unpublished MSW Thesis, School of Social Work, Louisiana State University, Baton Rouge, 1984.

6. D. S. Bridgman, *The Duration of Formal Education of High Ability Youth* (Washington, D.C.: National Science Foundation, 1961).

7. L. H. Fox, "Identification of the Academically Gifted," *American Psychologist*, 36, No. 10 (1981), pp. 1103–1111.

8. See, for example, J. R. Whitmore, *Identification of Highly Gifted Under-achievers at the Primary Level* (Kent, Ohio: Kent State University Press, 1982).

9. Ibid.

10. M. Fine and R. Pitts, "Intervention with Underachieving Gifted Children: Rationale and Strategies," *Gifted Child Quarterly*, 24 (Spring 1980), pp. 51–55.

11. B. Clark, *Growing Up Gifted* (Columbus, Ohio: Charles E. Merrill Publishing Co., 1979, pp. 279–286.

12. Webb, Meckstroth, and Tolan, *Guiding the Gifted Child*.

13. Ibid.

14. Ibid.

15. See, for example, M. Rotheram, "Social Skill Training with Under-achievers, Disruptive and Exceptional Children," *School Psychology*, 19, No. 3 (1982), pp. 532–537; J. Broedel, *A Study of the Effects of Group Counseling on the Academic Performance and Mental Health of Underachieving Gifted Adolescents* (Ann Arbor: University of Michigan Press, 1958); M. Ohlsen and C. Proff, *The Extent to Which Group Counseling Affects the Academic and Personal Adjustment of Underachieving Gifted Adolescents*, Cooperative Research Project No. 623(Washington, D.C.: U.S. Office of Education, 1960); F. Baymur and C. Patterson, "Three Methods of Assisting Underachieving High School Students," *Journal of Counseling Psychology*, 7 (1960), pp. 83–90; T. Mallison, *Gifted Underachievers* (Toronto, Canada: Board of Education, Research Department, 1972); and M. Zilli, "Reasons Why the Gifted Adolescent Underachieves and Some of the Implications of Guidance and Counseling to This Problem," *Gifted Child Quarterly*, 15 (1971), pp. 279–292.

16. Clark, *Growing Up Gifted*; and Fine and Pitts, "Intervention with Underachieving Gifted Children."

17. G. J. Manaster, *Adolescent Development and Life Tasks* (Boston: Allyn & Bacon, 1977).

18. A. P. Goldstein et al., *Skill Streaming the Adolescent* (Champaign, Ill.: Research Press Co., 1980).

Children with Handicaps: Transition from Preschool to School Programs

Elizabeth Floyd Gerlock

WELL-DEFINED PROCEDURES for coordinating a handicapped preschool child's move from an early intervention program to a school program assist the child's and family's adjustment to the new environment and the child's uninterrupted educational development. A child's entrance into the academic world at either the kindergarten or first-grade level is a major milestone in the life of any family. For the family with a child who is handicapped, this period may be one that underscores and reawakens the pain they felt when they learned their child was disabled. Their child may not be able to proceed as expected through this traditional rite of passage. Their hopes that their child would "catch up" in the early intervention program may be destroyed. If the child has not been in an early intervention program, going to school may be the first time parents have had to admit the extent of their child's problems.

Adding to the difficulties of this period is the failure of many preschool early intervention programs and schools to coordinate with each other. Preschool programs offer a nurturing environment for children and special services for parents, but they may pay insufficient attention to assessing the environment children will move to and preparing childen for that environment. They also may not educate parents about available options and the parents' role in transition. Schools have dedicated professionals who strive to provide a free appropriate education for all in accordance with

P. L. 94-142. However, they may pay too little attention to finding out what children have learned in preschool programs, teaching methods used, and successful strategies preschool teachers have discovered for working with children. Follow-up conferences between teachers may be nonexistent.

Families of normally developing children usually receive clear instructions regarding where these children will attend school, times and dates for enrollment, transportation arrangements, and what information is needed. Parents of children with handicaps often face confusion as to where their child can go to school, transportation arrangements, and what the necessary procedures are to get their children enrolled.

Experts in the field of early childhood special education agree that a carefully planned transition is crucial for a child to maintain the gains acquired in an early childhood program, but in actual practice good procedures are seldom employed.[1] A committee of the Tennessee Early Intervention Network for Children with Handicaps (TEINCH) decided to study the problem in Tennessee, explore practices and recommendations from programs and professionals who had focused on the issue, and formulate a set of practices that would ensure a smooth transition for preschool children with handicaps from preschool to school programs. TEINCH is composed of professionals and other interested persons from a variety of agencies and disciplines who identify problems in the provision of early intervention services in the state and seek to develop strategies to overcome these problems.

Transition Committee

Members of the Transition Committee included two teachers in early intervention programs, a special education teacher, both a preschool and a school social worker, three Head Start handicap services coordinators, a director of an advocacy agency, a principal of a public school serving children with handicaps, an outreach worker, and a preschool training coordinator. Committee activities were done in addition to members' regular work responsibilities. The committee conducted two surveys, which included 37 preschool programs and 20 administrators from both the preschool and the public school. Open-ended questions were used, with space to fill in the blanks. The committee also gained information by discussing problems and ways to provide a smooth transition in small groups at meetings that the Network held.

Survey Results

The preschool professionals were asked, "What are you doing that you find particularly helpful when (or before) children move from your program to the public school?" Most frequently mentioned (15 responses) was the multidisciplinary team (M-team) meeting, attended by both preschool and school personnel as well as parents, for developing the child's Individualized Educational Program (IEP). One response mentioned inviting the local education agency to participate in developing the preschool child's IEP the year before the child was ready to move into public school. The others referred to the M-team meeting when placement for a child was determined and the child was ready to move into the school system.

The second most often listed strategy (nine responses) was visits to possible school placements. Parental visits to school were mentioned most often, but one person recommended that children and preschool staff visit along with parents. One questionnaire discussed having school personnel observe the child in the preschool program.

Transfer of records, timely notification of schools regarding preschool children who would need special services, and special conferences between preschool and school personnel to share information about children who were moving from preschool to school programs were all listed on six responses.

Establishing good working relationships with the school system was a priority on five questionnaires. Contact between preschool and school teachers to share information and provide follow-up was listed four times. Providing parents with information about services available and parent rights were each cited three times. Less frequently given responses were as follows: parent meetings to provide transition information, establishing and clarifying transition procedures, having a representative from the school system on the preschool board of directors, providing preschool children with readiness activities and mainstreaming opportunities, and making sure children had needed assessments. These were all listed on two questionnaires. Listed once were having school teachers meet children and families in the child's home, providing information about financial resources for school, and helping parents work out transportation arrangements.

Another question the committee asked was, "What would you like to change about the way transition is now handled in your community?" Better communication and coordination with public school personnel was the most frequent response given. Three responses mentioned difficulty with confidentiality and poor procedures for securing parental permission. More involvement of the public school in earlier planning for children who would eventually enter public school and also planning for transition were felt to be needed. One response stated, "We have yet to develop a good relationship with the county school system. Would like to do so."

More parent education about their rights, the M-team and IEP process, and options available in the school were listed by three people as a need. One response asked that school personnel be more supportive: "Many parents have enjoyed good support and personal contact with staff and other parents in preschool programs—our introduction to a large, impersonal school system can be quite a shock. School personnel could often be more sensitive and helpful regarding this dimension of transition."

Letting parents know as far ahead as possible where children would be going to school and about special services and transportation arrangements were the ways three respondents would like things changed in their community. Another respondent asked for more information about P.L. 94-142 since a discrepancy existed between the preschool staff's understanding of the law and the school system's understanding. More consideration for the educational needs of children instead of fitting them into available programs and a program to handle multiply-handicapped children were changes two people would like to see in their communities. Preschool staff also wanted to see inservice for students, administrators, and teachers (including the regular education teachers as well as the special education teachers) who would be receiving the preschool children with disabilities.

The public school administrators, social workers, and special education consultants and supervisors pointed out some problems in how preschool programs were handling transition. They stressed the need for preschools to give them enough warning ahead of time about children with handicaps who would be coming to school. One response stated, "Sending teachers need to understand schools' programs and their goals. Parents need to be aware of differences in the preschool program and the school program."

Three public school respondents alluded to or discussed at length the problem of preschools presenting a negative picture of the public school. One director of education for the handicapped and gifted wrote, unfortunately sending agencies have sometimes taught parents to believe that they will have to fight for their children's rights in public school. So, parents sometimes come to us with a very defensive attitude. My first job is to try to develop trust with the parents and to make sure they understand their children's rights and our responsibility in relation to those rights.

Echoing the concern expressed by a preschool staff member regarding differences in understanding P.L. 94-142, a public school special education consultant stated,

many agencies and parents believe that they can request and must receive specific services, schools, programs, and/or teachers.... Services are provided according to need, not the wishes of others. Basically, services are provided to children with handicaps, not adults with special desires.

The same person found that lack of appropriate measures or procedures to identify handicapping conditions caused problems in transition.

Public school personnel stressed the need for communication, coordination, trust, cooperation, visits to new settings by parents and children, development of relationships between preschool and public school staff, and adequate preparation of children by preschool teachers. One supervisor of special education stated that providing program personnel time for transition procedures would "help eliminate many problems, misinterpretation, and misunderstanding." Clearly problems exist in Tennessee in regard to the way preschool staff that serve children with handicaps, public school staff, and parents communicate and cooperate with each other regarding children's move from preschool to school programs.

Preschool Analysis Project

The Preschool Analysis Project has done an extensive survey of 166 preschool programs that serve children with handicaps in Tennessee, examining practices in ten components of the programs.[2] Transition is the tenth component the project analyzed. Transition is defined as "preparing the family and the child to move to a new program, assisting in finding the appropriate placement, and remaining in contact with the family and the program's personnel after the changeover."

They found that 90 percent of the respondents assist parents in finding appropriate placements, but only 59 percent assign a specific person to assist the family with the transition. Of the programs surveyed, 56 percent do not arrange for the child to attend the new class on a trial basis, and 38 percent do not encourage the prospective teacher to observe the child in the current program. The Preschool Analysis Project further reported that follow-up/liaison activities are done the least comprehensively of all the transition activities. One-third to more than one-half of programs do not implement follow-up at all. These activities include continued formal and informal communication between the former and present teachers; complete systematic, written records at scheduled intervals; participation in formal meetings of involved personnel concerning the child's progress; and ongoing liaison services. Readiness training activities were the ones most often implemented.

Transition Projects across the Country

Recognizing the need for improvement in transition services for preschool children with handicaps, Special Education and Rehabilitative Services, United States Department of Education, and other agencies have funded projects across the country to develop models for good transition practices. The TEINCH Transition Committee corresponded with many of these programs and collected materials the programs have developed.

In Houston, Texas, Project Transition developed and field-tested a parent notebook.[3] This notebook provides information and plans for a series of five parent meetings to prepare families for their child's move from preschool programs to school programs.

At the University of Washington in Seattle, the Single Portal Intake Project and the Regional Interagency Center have developed a systematic set of procedures to ensure a child's smooth transition including suggested timelines.[4]

Paine and Fowler have a paper on transition distributed through the University of Kansas Early Childhood Institute.[5] Fowler also has a published chapter on transition.[6] The emphasis is on the classroom adjustment of children with behavior or learning problems. While some of these children's problems may have improved considerably in the special preschool classrooms, gains will be lost unless the children are taught the skills they will need in the next classroom and both classrooms cooperate in planning for the move and continue contact during the children's adjustment to the new classroom. The emphasis in the two papers is on children who move to a mainstreamed setting.

Project TIMMI (Training and Intervention to Multihandicapped Mothers and Infants), Petersburg, Virginia, reported on an evaluation of their transition model prepared for them by the Evaluation Research Center, School of Education, University of Virginia.[7] Twenty transition activities were carried out as a result of the needs assessment of the community regarding problems with transition. The evaluation showed considerable improvement in parents', teachers', and supervisors' satisfaction with the way the transition occurred over the previous year before the activities were implemented. Moreover, the project noted their satisfaction with the model for attacking the transition problem in their community using a process and problem-solving approach.

Transition Brochure

In order to increase awareness in Tennessee of good transition practices, the TEINCH Transition Committee applied for and received a small grant to develop and print a brochure. The brochure contains checklists for administrators, sending teachers, receiving teachers, and parents. With the assistance of several Tennessee state departments and other agencies, 3800 copies of the brochure were printed and distributed.[8] The checklists and accompanying comments are included below.

Administrators

Both preschool and school administrators have the responsibility to set a tone of cooperation and willingness to work together. They have the responsibility for making sure that procedures are established that will coordinate the efforts of all those who are seeking to provide needed services for children with handicaps and their families.

Suggested Checklist for Administrators

_____ Make sure "child-find"—identifying and locating preschool children who are to begin their regular schooling—is ongoing.

_____ Share information about children who are ready to move on as early as possible.

_____ Designate a contact person to handle transition

_____ Provide release time for teachers to visit preschool or school programs.

_____ Provide teachers with time for follow-up contacts.

_____ Be sure parents and teachers are in touch with each other and are receiving all necessary information. Keep information flowing.

_____ Share services and materials between preschools and schools as appropriate.

_____ Set up staffings or M-team meetings. Include sending and receiving teachers.

_____ Provide parents with information about their children's rights and their rights.

_____ Follow state regulations in accordance with P.L. 94-142 in placing children.

_____ Provide parents with a list of information that the school needs about their children.

Provide parents with training opportunities on how to be involved in school and how to express concerns.

_____ Learn about the preschool or school programs in the community.

_____ Be sure children have appropriate diagnostic tests and assessments of progress to ensure placement and continued progress.

_____ Whenever possible, provide placement and programming options for children and families.

Sending Teachers

Sending teachers have had the opportunity to learn about children's learning styles, strengths, and weaknesses and to determine what support services are needed. They have had opportunities to establish rapport with parents and develop an understanding of their needs and concerns. They can help prepare both children and parents for moving on.

Suggested Checklist for Sending Teachers

_____ Keep good records of evaluations, children's progress, and successful teaching strategies.

_____ Visit school classrooms.

_____ Teach children social, self-help, and group skills that they will need in the next environment.

_____ Provide the school with information about children who will be coming.

_____ Get parents to sign release of information forms for information to be sent to schools.

_____ Provide parents with a copy of school records and encourage them to keep a notebook or file.

_____ Meet informally with receiving teachers.

_____ Support and document requests made to the school for services.

_____ Help determine the most appropriate and least restrictive placement.

_____ Provide reassurance, support, and guidance for families and children.

_____ Complete a short information form to provide receiving teachers with pertinent information as soon as the children's new placements are determined.

_____ Convey a positive attitude.

_____ Remain in touch with receiving teachers during the year to provide follow-up consultation.

Receiving Teachers
The receiving teachers help children maintain the progress they have made in the preschool and continue to develop more skills and greater independence. Through their contact with parents and sending teachers, the receiving teachers learn more about children's achievements and what problems children are experiencing. They make the transition easier by being flexible in their expectations and plans for new students.

Suggested Checklist for Receiving Teachers

_____ Visit preschool programs to observe classroom procedures and teaching strategies and to learn about curriculum and support services.

_____ Plan an open house for preschool parents and children to see the school program.

_____ Get acquainted with parents of children coming to your classes before school starts with either a phone call or a visit. Find out about parents' expectations for their children.

_____ Provide parents with a packet of information about the school, including teacher's name, transportation arrangements, and meal arrangements.

_____ Review all records on the children maintained by the preschools.

_____ Attend multidisciplinary team conferences with the sending teachers to learn about children's strengths and weaknesses. Include them in M-team meetings for the children.

_____ Prepare children in a mainstreamed classroom for the child with a disability.

_____ Provide emotional support and, if possible, refer parents to support groups.

_____ Be flexible in planning for children and parents.

_____ Continue to confer with sending teachers during the year about children's progress and problems.

_____ Provide suggestions to help sending teachers prepare children for school classrooms.

_____ Arrange for appropriate related services.

Parents

Parents know their children better than anyone else does. They need a balance of caution along with optimism in planning for their children's futures. They need to learn to work with professionals, being open to diagnoses and prognoses but continuing to evaluate the information given in light of their knowledge of the children's development.

Parents usually become experts in their knowledge about their children's disabilities. They also need to be experts in their knowledge about their children's educational rights, including the provisions of P.L. 94-142, the multidisciplinary team (M-team), and their children's Individualized Educational Program (IEP). Parents are the ones who seek a match between services available or potentially available in their community and the services their children need. When participating in staffings, parents should be confident about the contribution they have to make based on their knowledge about, concern for, and love of their children. When an educational program is not satisfactory, parents need to know how to work with the school to seek changes.

Parents also have the responsibility to balance their own needs and those of their families with the needs of their children who have handicaps. In some cases, parents will have to evaluate suggestions for additional services for their children in terms of their overall family situations. Other parents who have children with handicaps may be able to provide them with support and encouragement either informally or through parent support groups. Seeking help when difficulties arise is an indication of strength, not of weakness.

The checklist below will assist parents to be prepared for their children's transition from preschool programs to public school programs.

Suggested Checklist for Parents

_____ Request copies of all reports of evaluations, teachers' summaries, and medical reports on your child.

_____ Keep a file or notebook of all records on your child including the following:

    _____ Doctors' reports

    _____ Teachers' reports

    _____ Diagnostic evaluations

    _____ Record of immunizations

_____ Ask questions about any reports you don't understand.

_____ Learn about the provisions of P.L. 94-142 for your child's education, including the following:

    _____ Individualized Education Program (IEP)

    _____ Multidisciplinary team (M-team)

    _____ Related services

    _____ Least restrictive environment

    _____ Your right to refuse to sign the IEP and to call an M-team meeting

    _____ Your right to access to your child's records

_____ Visit school programs available for your child.

_____ Provide the school with records required, including records of:

    _____ Physical examinations

    _____ Immunizations

    _____ Certification of specific disability from appropriate medical specialist

    _____ Records of diagnostic evaluations

_____ Inform school of all previous services your child has received.

_____ Make choices for your child's education based on all available information: evaluations, preschool performance, knowledge of your child, and professional advice.

_____ Get to know the receiving teacher as early as possible.

_____ Participate in staffings and be confident in your knowledge of your child.

_____ Know how to work with the school to seek changes in your child's educational program when needed.

Role of the Social Worker

School or preschool social workers may be the ideal persons in a community to take the responsibility to assess concerns regarding transition procedures and, when needed, to help develop better communication for coordination and cooperation between agencies. Social workers are often the persons who provide coordination between agencies and are in contact with children and families. Recognizing the importance of this period for maintaining and continuing children's progress and for avoiding unnecessary trauma for families, social workers can assist community professionals in setting aside the time needed to plan smooth transitions for children and families.

Notes and References

1. P. Hutinger, "Transition Practices for Handicapped Young Children: What the Experts Say," *Journal of the Division for Early Childhood,* 2 (April 1981), pp. 8–14.

2. "Preschool Analysis Project Report #7: Analysis of Components Comprising Tennessee Preschool Programs for Handicapped and High Risk Children Birth to Six Years of Age," 1 (November 9, 1984), Program Evalua-

tion Lab, John F. Kennedy Center of Vanderbilt University, and Tennessee Children's Services Commission, Nashville. (Photocopied.)

3. "Project Transition Parent Notebook," Infant Programs, Mental Health/Mental Retardation Authority of Harris County, Houston, Tex., 1981. (Photocopied.)

4. Child Development and Mental Retardation Center, "The Early Childhood Interagency Transition Model: Strategy Outline" (Seattle: College of Education, University of Washington, November 1981). (Photocopied.)

5. S. C. Paine and S. A. Fowler, "Helping Young Handicapped Children Succeed When They Enter Public School," Practical Paper Series (Lawrence: Kansas Early Childhood Institute, University of Kansas, undated). (Photocopied.)

6. S. A. Fowler, "Transition from Preschool to Kindergarten for Children with Special Needs," in K. E. Allen et al., eds., *Early Childhood Education: Special Problems, Special Solutions* (Rockville, Md.: Aspen Publications, 1982).

7. Evaluation Research Center, "Developing Transition Approaches Between Infant Intervention and Preschool Programs for the Handicapped: An Interim Evaluation Report for Project TIMMI [Training and Intervention to Multihandicapped Mothers and Infants, Petersburg, Va.]" (Charlottesville: School of Education, University of Virginia, January 1983). (Photocopied.)

8. The state departments and other agencies included Mental Health/ Mental Retardation, Education, Health and Environment, Children's Services Commission, Center for Training and Technical Assistance, and EACH (Effective Advocacy for Citizens with Handicaps).

Forming Partnerships with Families of Handicapped Children

Donna S. Swall
Forrest L. Swall

FAMILIES TOGETHER, INC., a nonprofit organization formed in Lawrence, Kansas, in 1982, is an exciting and practical way to serve vital but often unmet needs of families with handicapped children. The original idea for Families Together, Inc., came from a special education teacher in Kansas, who was able to hear the needs of families expressed in so many different ways by the parents of children in her class for the severely and multiply handicapped. What she heard was that these parents felt different, isolated, and lacking support; they felt unable for a variety of reasons to do what they sensed families without handicapped children could do so easily. She felt their frustration with the relentless daily stress of caring for their handicapped children while still trying to meet their own needs and the needs of their other children.[1]

Families Together was created to help strengthen and support families with handicapped children by providing group experiences in recreation, education, and sharing for the entire family. These experiences are provided through a unique service delivery model called the Family Enrichment Weekend.

This article has three main purposes: (1) to propose that a successful Families Together program can be a contributing factor in achieving educational excellence for handicapped children; (2) to explore the far-ranging effect of creative partnerships in meeting the needs of families with handicapped children; and (3) to explore

33

the role of school social workers in taking responsibility for developing creative partnerships for meeting the needs of families with handicapped children.

The Problem

Families with a developmentally disabled member encounter high levels of stress associated with the care of the disabled member. These effects in families are well documented.[2] The effects include severe marital disharmony in approximately one-third of the families with developmentally disabled children.[3] Disharmony is viewed as a consequence of the added financial costs, social isolation, limitations in recreational activities, stigma, additional time spent in the personal care of the child, difficulty in handling problem behavior, interrupted sleep, difficulty in carrying out normal household routines, and pessimistic views of the future.[4]

Other problems families encounter involve taking vacations, participating in community activities, locating babysitters, providing complicated diets or treatments, extra housework, and maladjustment in siblings.[5] The added stress experienced by these families is a possible cause of the disproportionate number of developmentally disabled children who are victims of child abuse.[6]

The Program

The Families Together program is most visible in the enrichment weekend experience. Three less visible components of the program are follow-up support, referral services, and student training.

The Family Enrichment Weekend

The enrichment weekend is a gathering of 18 to 20 families, each with a disabled child, who spend a weekend learning and recreating together. Families of assorted sizes and makeup attend, including single parents, foster and adoptive parents, parents and grandparents, aunts and uncles, and the handicapped child or children with their siblings. The weekend begins at 9:00 A.M. on Saturday and ends at 3:00 or 4:00 P.M. on Sunday.

Small-Group Discussions.   One of the major activities or events during a weekend is discussions between parents and volunteer resource persons around a range of issues identified ahead of time by the parents, including (1) use of inner resources—examining personal stress and burnout; (2) growing up and leaving home—

examining group homes and vocational training in your area; (3) working with professionals—how to be an equal member of the team; (4) "the Individualized Educational Program and you"—knowing your rights; (5) planning your financial future; and (6) foster care, respite care, and out-of-home placement. The resource persons include professionals from various disciplines, legislators, and others whose interests or expertise are compatible with the needs expressed by the parents.

Children's Activities.   Learning groups and recreation adapted to the ages and needs of the disabled children and their siblings are a central part of the program. Also, nonhandicapped brothers and sisters have the chance to get to know other children and share their special concerns with each other.

Family Recreation and Leisure Activities.   Using volunteer professional instructors, families have an opportunity to broaden their knowledge about family-centered activities.

An Evening Out for Parents.   Volunteer sitters mind the children while parents go out. This activity provides parents with an evening free of child care responsibilities with the assurance that their children are in competent and caring hands.

Making New Friends.   Parents have opportunities to relax, play, and learn from others who share similar accomplishments and concerns.

Follow-Up Support

The experiences of the weekend provide staff and families with an opportunity to know each other. This is particularly useful when follow-up service such as respite care, ongoing family contact, and referrals are needed.

Student Training

Sixty to 75 volunteers provide 1,000 volunteer hours with the children each enrichment weekend. The students come from area colleges and universities, such as Washburn University, Topeka; Baker University, Baldwin; Emporia State University, Emporia; and the University of Kansas, Lawrence. The students are enrolled in a variety of professional programs, such as special education, music therapy, speech therapy, early childhood development, human development and family life, occupational therapy, physical therapy, and social work.

During the weekend, student volunteers receive instruction and supervision in working with children with varied disabilities. The students spend the major part of the weekend with their assigned families. Following the weekend, students have the opportunity to provide respite care for their families.

Several university instructors have begun to use the enrichment weekend as a laboratory for fulfillment of class assignments. The student and in-service training resource, including internship and field practicum assignments in the Families Together program, has only begun to be utilized.

High school students, service club members, and other members of the community who are interested in families with disabled children also serve as volunteers at enrichment weekends. Their experience and training contribute to developing awareness and attitude changes in the community, other dimensions of creative partnerships.

Resource Center

Another service of Families Together is the 24-hour telephone resource. Parents and others may seek information and advice about any facet of family life or any need relating to particular family situations, ranging from finding competent sitters to advocating for a given child in the school and the community. Parents receive support and encouragement in matters of placement and programming.

Parents have secured financial assistance for equipment, professional consultation, and preschool programming for their handicapped child through the resource center. Staff persons are available to accompany parents on visits to agencies, when requested. The resource center staff remain in contact with parents until the situation is resolved or the parent is able to continue independently.

Service Dimensions

Eligibility

Referrals may come from any source including families themselves. Families are registered for Family Enrichment Weekends on a first-come, first-served basis. An intake process is used for gathering pertinent information about family needs so that individualized programming can take place.

Administration and Service Delivery

Families Together is essentially a volunteer organization. Board members include parents of disabled children as well as persons representing a range of professional disciplines related to children with handicapped conditions. Parents, professionals, and other interested persons serve as volunteer staff for enrichment weekends.

At the present time, the executive director serves without compensation. She is a special education teacher with more than ten years of experience working with severely and multiply handicapped children. Long-range plans call for two paid staff members, an executive director and a program coordinator, one of whom will be a parent of a handicapped child.

Financing

The costs of the program are incurred primarily during the enrichment weekends conducted at an accessible hotel, such as the Holiday Inn Holidome in Lawrence. The cost per family is approximately $300. Three enrichment weekends yearly, with 20 families at each weekend, require approximately $18,000 per year. Funding for the program is accomplished in the following ways:

Participating Families. Financially able families pay as much of the $300 as possible. In 1984, one-third of the families paid part of the fee, which amounted to an income of $3,000. No family has paid more than half of the weekend cost.

Individuals and Organizations. Approximately 25 organizations, such as church groups, professional societies, and service clubs, are regular contributors to Families Together. These organizational as well as individual contributions are generated through personal contacts made by the executive director, other board members, and friends of families who have participated in enrichment weekends.

Foundations. Grants or contributions from foundations and area businesses provide about one-third of the costs of the annual program. Low overhead due to the volunteer nature of the organization is appealing to many foundations. Thus, the potential for additional foundation grants is good, and the board is pursuing this avenue for long-range support.

United Way Support. The Lawrence United Way has designated Families Together as a member agency, providing $2,700 in 1984 and $4,000 in 1985. This money can be used for Lawrence/Douglas County families only. Again, since families attend from other areas of Kansas, other local United Way organizations are another funding source to pursue.

Fund-Raising Activities. These activities, which were started prior to United Way support, constitute a small but important part of the financing of enrichment weekends. In 1984, the sale of terry cloth "Famtog" Easter basket bunnies, other handicrafts designed specifically for Families Together, and a concentrated laundry detergent netted approximately $500, enough to cover the expenses of two families participating in an enrichment weekend.

Creative Partnerships

The concept of partnerships is not new to social workers, especially to school social workers, who every day renew and revitalize their partnerships with the primary actors in the host setting of the school. Families Together has developed a series of creative partnerships, which began with the collaboration between a Kansas teacher of severely and multiply handicapped children and the parents of those children.

At an early stage in the development of the idea of bringing families together for recreation and renewal, the special education teacher made contact with a social work couple in Lawrence. Their first role was to serve as a sounding board for her as she worked at fleshing out this original idea. Their major role was to support the teacher's genuine commitment to families of handicapped children, again a vital partnership for the continued evolution of her dream to meet a real need of the families whose children she served in her special education classroom. Social work knowledge of family dynamics and social work values relating to families made enthusiastic support of such an idea natural.

School social workers, because of their specialized function in the schools, their regular contacts with families whose children receive special education services, and their unique home–school–community liaison role, are well-prepared to develop partnerships with and for families of disabled children and with those in the community whose resources helped make the idea of Families Together a reality. Specifically, these partnerships have included the following:

1. Partnerships with parents of handicapped children in order to develop together the programs and services that meet their needs most effectively.

2. Partnerships with various professional people (that is, mental health practitioners, Association for Retarded Citizens, Council for Exceptional Children, and college faculty) to make use of their expertise in planning weekend workshops and in serving as resource persons and consultants to families in the weekend experiences.

3. Partnerships with local business, service, and church groups to obtain necessary financial support and to achieve greater community awareness of family needs.

4. Partnerships with college students and community volunteers to serve as companions for the handicapped children and their nonhandicapped siblings at the weekend events.

5. Partnerships with the local news media to publicize the activities.

6. Partnerships with the convention hotel staff to create the necessary special arrangements, including special weekend rates, to accommodate families with handicapped children.

These partnerships and others have been instrumental in making the enrichment weekends possible, but their value extends beyond the family enrichment weekends. Such partnerships have potential value for achieving educational excellence for handicapped children everywhere.

Implications for School Social Workers

Social workers in the schools are in a unique position to facilitate partnerships with and for families of handicapped children. School social workers and professionals from other human service disciplines know that tremendous stress exists in families with handicapped children and that this stress often interferes with success in school. Neither social workers, other professionals, nor the families can accomplish by themselves the task of meeting the needs that contribute to this stress. However, through the potential of partnerships, the task of meeting the needs of families with handicapped children can be undertaken. Families can be helped to cope, and families can be strengthened and experience enrichment through partnerships extended throughout the community. As these partnerships are nurtured and maintained, essential and appropriate social, health, and educational services will be assured. A major reward in these partnerships can be educational excellence for children.

Notes and References

1. The special education teacher was Chris Curry, who thought that the families of the children in her classes could draw strength and hope from

an opportunity for recreation, learning, and sharing with other families who had handicapped children. In Curry's discussions with other professionals, an idea began to take shape for a planned weekend get-together for a small number of families in an accessible convention-style hotel, so that the participating families along with their handicapped children could have a mini-vacation together. Edwin A. Helmstetter, who at that time was Project Coordinator, Curriculum Project for Deaf-Blind Youth, University of Kansas, did the literature search identifying family stress that this program was designed to alleviate.

2. B. Farber, "Family Adaptations to Severely Mentally Retarded Children," in M. J. Begab and S. A. Richardson, eds., *The Mentally Retarded and Society: A Social Science Perspective* (Baltimore, Md.: University Park Press, 1975), pp. 247–266; J. B. Fotheringham, M. Skelton, and B. A. Hoddinott, "The Effects on the Family of the Presence of a Mentally Retarded Child," *Canadian Psychiatric Association Journal*, 17, No. 3 (1972), pp. 283–289; and W. N. Friedrich and W. L. Friedrich; "Psychosocial Assets of Parents of Handicapped and Nonhandicapped Children," *American Journal of Mental Deficiency*, 85, No. 5 (1981), pp. 551–553.

3. A. Gath, "The Impact of an Abnormal Child Upon the Parents," *British Journal of Psychiatry*, 130 (1977), pp. 405–410.

4. R. M. Moroney, "Public Social Policy: Impact on Families with Handicapped Children," in J. L. Paul, ed., *Understanding and Working with Parents of Children with Special Needs* (New York: Holt, Rinehart & Winston, 1981).

5. B. Farber and D. B. Ryckman, "Effects of Severely Mentally Retarded Children on Family Relationships," *Mental Retardation Abstracts*, 2 (January–March 1965), pp. 1–17; G. Travis, *Chronic Illness: Its Impact on Child and Family* (Stanford, Calif.: Stanford University Press, 1976); and A. Gath, "The School Age Sibling of Mongol Children," *British Journal of Psychiatry*, 123 (1973), pp. 161–167.

6. L. H. Embry, "Family Support for Handicapped Preschool Children at Risk for Abuse," in J. J. Gallagher, ed., *New Directions for Exceptional Children: Parents and Families of Handicapped Children*, Vol. 4 (San Francisco: Jossey-Bass, 1980), pp. 29–57.

Chronic Sorrow: Plight of Parents of Special Children

Marie Rothschild

THERE ARE TWO SCHOOLS of thought in the literature about the reaction of parents of mentally handicapped children to the tragedy that befalls their families. One is that parents work through their grief over time; the other is that sorrow is chronic.[1] Some theoreticians claim that grief is time bound and that parents go through stages of grief in the order of shock, despair, guilt, withdrawal, acceptance, and, finally, adjustment. As I see it, this description of feelings is appropriate in describing the initial period of mourning when the child is first diagnosed as handicapped and enrolled in a school for handicapped children. When you have the opportunity to follow a family after the preschool stage of the handicapped child, you become aware of the chronicity of the problem. Acceptance has to do with accepting the fact that the child will always be handicapped because he or she is developmentally delayed; adjustment means continual adjusting to the chronic nature of the child's problem and the need for the help of professionals at various times throughout the child's life.

I hold the theory, expressed by Olshansky, of "chronic sorrow" as the description of the responses of parents of handicapped children.[2] Olshansky agrees that initial shock and a period of acute grieving takes place; however, there are many times thereafter that the intense feelings of grieving are reevoked and experienced. It is particularly important for the social worker to accept the idea that chronic sorrow is a natural, rather than neurotic, reaction. Having a handicapped child should be viewed as a tragedy rather than a parental psychiatric problem. At various times throughout the child's life, it is important to be available to clarify the legitimacy of parental problems.

Chronic sorrow is caused by the nature of the prolonged burden of care.[3] Parents of normal children also experience many woes, trials, and despair. Most of the time, however, they know that ultimately the child will become a self-sufficient adult. By contrast, the parents of a mentally defective child have little to look forward to; they will always be burdened by the child's unrelenting demands and unabated dependency.

These parents are acutely aware of their own mortality even when they are relatively young. Their interest in wills and trusts is keen because of their awareness of the importance of who is chosen to be the guardian of their trust. They often have to deal with the ambivalence of the chosen guardian.

Parents grow older and their needs change, but the dependency needs of the child remain constant. One parent told me that she has been listening to "Sesame Street" for 16 years, and she refuses to do it for another day, even though her 16-year-old retarded child still enjoys it.

Goals of the Social Worker

The goals in counseling must be twofold: to increase the parents' acceptance of living with and adjusting to their defective child and to help the parents develop the tools they need to increase the skills of their handicapped child by translating the processes of children's education to parents. In addition to specific adaptive skills, social workers dealing with parents may also focus on more general problems of behavior management, such as discipline issues and parent-child communication.[4]

Parents of normal children have their own histories as a model for normal development. Parents of handicapped children need to learn from professionals to help the child through stages. The professionals are able to interpret the assessment of the child's abilities into possible behavioral changes; they can translate diagnostic terms into realistic expectations of the child. The special educators, speech therapists, and psychologists are able to share their knowledge with the parents. The social workers then can help parents follow through with the difficult tasks suggested.

The personal impact on the professional is powerful when he or she begins to work with the parents of handicapped children. The parents' pain is sometimes overwhelming, and the chronicity often gives one the feeling of hopelessness.

In order to be an effective social worker, a reexamination of one's own feelings and attitudes must occur. The social worker may feel guilty, possibly because he or she is relieved that the misfortune fell upon someone else. If the social worker is not aware of this reaction, he or she will be unable to deal constructively with the parents' anger and frustration. Few persons can view a small child who is handicapped without feeling grief. Acceptance of this reaction in oneself and skillful handling of it can enhance the worker's approach to these families.[5] Sometimes, feelings of one's own losses are reawakened, which often causes personal pain. But, the awareness of those feelings in oneself can help the worker empathize with the feelings of loss and grief felt by the parents.

Task for the Social Worker

At the Herbert G. Birch School for Exceptional Children, we have designed a unique program to try to satisfy the myriad needs of parents with handicapped children. The Herbert G. Birch School has a day program that serves handicapped children between the ages of 5 and 16 years. There is also a preschool program for children aged 2 to 4 years, 9 months. The children in both programs present a variety of handicapping conditions, including: neurological impairment, autism, mental retardation, learning disabilities, speech-language impairment, and emotional disturbance. The program is based on a behavior modification approach, and staff function within an interdisciplinary team framework.

We have found that ongoing services to families are very important. Most of the literature in social work journals revolves around the crisis period at the initial shock of diagnosis-prognosis, when intervention is critical. However, the chronicity of the problems necessitates ongoing intervention, as the inevitable crises occur throughout the lives of these parents.[6]

At Birch, each family is assigned a social worker who acts as a case manager. For purposes of this article, I will discuss only the families who avail themselves of the full complement of services: individual or marital counseling, group counseling, and a community organization group provided by the social worker. Additionally, there are educational workshops provided by special educators, speech and language therapists, and psychologists. Parent participation in the services does not seem to be limited to one type of parent. Rather, participants cross economic class groupings (except for welfare recipients, who are reluctant to participate) as well as levels of education. Lack of participation seems to relate to parents' past experiences with professionals, the degree to which parents are ready to deal with the severity of the problems, or circumstances in their lives irrespective of the handicapped child, such as welfare recipients' concentration on survival rather than quality of life.

The social worker who takes a generic or multimethod approach to practice has available a repertoire of professional practice methods from which to select, including working with individuals, total families, or subsections; groups of unrelated people; and communities.[7] The difference in our work is that we are using a simultaneous three-pronged approach, which is usually contraindicated. When working with families of handicapped children, however, it is prescribed. The traditional view of group counseling is that the therapeutic intervention is not life but rather a rehearsal for life. The group at the Herbert G. Birch School is based on life as we deal with the issue of chronic sorrow. The usual issues of competitiveness among group members for workers' attention seem to diminish because of mutual empathy.[8] Therefore, the usual rivalry does not exist, which makes it preferable for the same worker to perform each service. The individual work complements and supports the work of the group.

An example of this phenomenon is the day that I told one group member, individually, that the staff had suggested that she see me individually again for a short time to work on some problems specifically related to her child's recent negative behavior. She was irate. She felt that it was an unfair demand after two years of individual work. She said she would have to discuss it with the group. The following group session was remarkable. The members were supportive of her feelings, were able to express their anger toward me for pointing out the parent's weakness, and then moved toward supporting the idea because they thought it was necessary, even though they are all tired of working with and for their children after ten years and identified with the group member in question.

The relationship that is established between the worker and the family is built on trust, enabling the two to withstand the changes in role on the part of the worker during each type of encounter. Due to their extensive problems, the clients seem to prefer working with one worker in the three modalities because of the worker's knowledge of the idiosyncratic factors relating to their families and the peculiar demands of their handicapped children.

We find group work particularly effective with parents and siblings. The mutual support and sharing of feelings and experiences becomes invaluable at many junctures along the way. The beginning parent groups share their grief, finding solace in sharing with the only others they know who have similar feelings of mourning. As the group stays together, recurring themes are dealt with, such as: reestablishing family priorities, attempting to pay attention to marital problems, considering forgotten siblings, and the individual parent's feelings of self-worth that have often been maligned.[9]

At the onset of the handicapped child's adolescence, many of the parent's original feelings come to the fore. The intense feelings of mourning reappear when normal milestones come and go unmarked in the life of the handicapped. For example, religious rituals such as Catholic confirmations and Jewish Bar/Bat Mitzvahs cause particular grief to many parents. The celebration of a girl's sixteenth birthday as a mark of "coming of age" has become a middle-class tradition. This kind of celebration is usually not possible for families whose children are handicapped. It is at times like these that the worker should be aware of the dangers of prolonged periods of mourning or melancholia. Freud defines mourning as a reaction to the loss of a loved one or a similar abstraction; melancholia is a sustained state of mourning when one's interest in the outside world wanes and one turns away from any activity not related to the loss.[10] Just as the worker worked toward acceptance of the chronicity of the sorrow at other times, so too during the adolescent stage we try to help the parents accept what is, while we deal with the feelings of anger and grief that are evoked. It is important for the worker to encourage parents to face the anger they have toward the handicapped child. If the parents "protect" the child by failing to reveal their anger toward him or her, the child will tend to act in an infantile manner both with parents and with other people. The child will not have been helped to learn what kind of behavior is acceptable both at home and in the outside world.[11] Feeling angry toward those one loves is a common emotional reaction, as is guilt following the anger. For parents of handicapped children, however, those feelings of guilt are usually magnified, which prevents expressions of anger.

As a tool for evaluating the work of the social worker in the group, a questionnaire has been designed as an instrument to measure growth.[12] The questions relate to the group members' participation in activities not related to their involvement with their handicapped child. The social worker will answer the questionnaire several times during the school year, and then its results will be evaluated at the end of the year.

Individual or family counseling is used to enhance the work of the group in dealing with the impact of the handicapped child on each family. Often we find that couples who might have been able to withstand the rigors of life together without the help of a professional need help with the familial relationships due to the trauma caused by the handicapping conditions. Siblings are often ignored during the entire first phase of diagnosis, and, as a matter of fact, there is very little research available to measure the effects of a handicapped child on siblings.[13] Certainly all children react differently, and there are many variables that affect normal children. However, knowing about the stress provoked by the handicapped child, we offer a sibling group each year, which is very well received. The mere fact that the parent is going out of the way to drive the sibling to the school of the handicapped child, just for the benefit of the sibling, gives an intrinsic value to the group before the child even participates.

The community organization group, in the form of a parent association, works for the mental health of the parents. It enables the parents to work through some of their feelings of inadequacy and discomfort in being "clients," by working as concerned citizens in service to the school to provide information for parents, steps toward advocacy, and fund raising. The social worker's role in this group is one of adviser, facilitator, advocate, and liaison with school authorities. This differs greatly from the role of leader in the counseling group. The group holds two meetings each month; the first is a meeting of the executive committee that presides over the parent association at both sites, and the second is a general information meeting for all parents.

Education

Education regarding parenting of a handicapped child is another area that must be addressed in all three modalities. Normal children grow like flowers, learning from the nurturing of their environment. Handicapped children need to be taught everything: to speak, to use language to communicate appropriately, to play, to separate from the mother, ad infinitum. The parent has to play the role of teacher in areas such as self-help and social skills. The social worker can act as consultant in helping to transfer skills learned by the child at school into the home. Parent participation is vital in acquiring such skills as toilet training, language acquisition, play, dressing and feeding skills, attention focusing, and imitation.

Summary

To emphasize the premise of this article, I will summarize by describing the work with one group over a span of ten years, using the three modalities simultaneously—individual counseling, group counseling, and community organization—to combat chronic sorrow. When children enter our preschool program, parents participate in an orientation group, which develops into a mothers' group. The mothers' group deals with acute feelings of mourning and grief. At the same time, workshops are offered to teach parents the techniques of behavior modification and of helping the child speak and develop language. This particular group of mothers, after two years, became the core of an evening parent group that has continued, in different forms, over the years.

The parent group spent years working through feelings of anger and guilt revolving around the handicapped child. At different times, group members would see the worker individually, or as couples, to work through their unique problems. The group went on to tackle marital problems that affect the handicapped child, and the focus became one of concentrating on individual needs and those of other loved ones, other than the handicapped child.

Several members of the parent group became the spearheads for organizing a parent association. In that milieu, they dealt with the apathy of others and the difficulties of getting an organization off the ground. They worked hard at developing a program and involving other parents.

The counseling group continued, some years meeting weekly and some years every other week. Its focus has taken a different turn again during the children's emerging adolescence. By this time, the parents have developed a grudging acceptance of the reality of the chronicity of the handicapping condition. Now the issues are separation and independence. Of course, separation and independence is the agenda of all adolescents. However, parents of handicapped children have to do the separating for themselves and their children—an extremely difficult task. As it is for parents of normal children, adolescence is a time when one's old anxieties resurface. However, for parents of handicapped children, the chronic sorrow becomes acute again, and many of the issues dealt with during preschool days crop up again, and parents' needs become intense. At this point, the counseling group continues to be a valuable tool for the worker. The following quote from a parent describes the dynamic nature of the group:

> Thinking, exploring our thoughts,
> Touching and accepting our feelings,
> Together helping, understanding,
> Reaching out to one another.

Notes and References

1. L. Wikler, M. Wasow, and E. Hatfield, "Chronic Sorrow Revisited: Parent vs. Professional Depiction of the Adjustment of Parents of Mentally Retarded Children," *American Journal of Orthopsychiatry*, 51 (January 1981), pp. 63–70.

2. S. Olshansky, "Chronic Sorrow: A Response to Having a Mentally Defective Child," *Social Casework*, 43 (April 1962), pp. 190–193.

3. L. Wikler, "Chronic Stresses of Families of Mentally Retarded Children," in Wikler and M. P. Keenan, eds., *Developmental Disabilities: No Longer a Private Tragedy* (Washington, D.C.: National Association of Social Workers, 1983), pp. 102–110.

4. E. K. Proctor, "New Directions for Work with Parents of Retarded Children," *Social Casework*, 57 (April 1976), pp. 259–264.

5. P. C. Cohen, "The Impact of the Handicapped Child on the Family," *Social Casework*, 43 (March 1972), pp. 137–142.

6. S. Schild, "Beyond Diagnosis: Issues in Recurrent Counseling of Parents of the Mentally Retarded," *Social Work in Health Care*, 8 (Fall 1982), pp. 81–93.

7. M. E. Hartford, "Group Methods and Generic Practice," in R. W. Roberts and H. Northen, eds., *Theories of Social Work with Groups* (New York: Columbia University Press, 1976).

8. M. Seitz, Professor of Social Work, Adelphi University, Garden City, N.Y., Consultant to Variety Pre-schoolers Workshop, December 1984.

9. S. T. Cummings, "The Impact of the Child's Deficiency on the Father: A Study of Fathers of Mentally Retarded and of Chronically Ill Children," *American Journal of Orthopsychiatry*, 46 (April 1976), pp. 246–255.

10. S. Freud, "Mourning and Melancholia" (1917), *General Psychological Theory* (New York: Macmillan, 1963).

11. Cohen, "The Impact of the Handicapped Child on the Family."

12. M. Bortner, Professor of Psychology, Yeshiva University, New York City, Consultant to Herbert G. Birch School, January 1984.

13. F. Trevino, "Siblings of Handicapped Children: Identifying Those at Risk," in Wikler and Keenan, eds., *Developmental Disabilities*, pp. 133–138.

A Support System for Parents with Learning-Disabled Children

Harry K. Dillard
Beverly Donenberg
Harriet Glickman

"I LIKED THE FEELING of not being isolated" "It's nice to know that there are other people in the same boat." "Sharing experiences with other parents is great." These statements typified the parents' evaluation of a support group led by a school social worker and a learning disabilities teacher.

The impetus to initiate parent support groups developed over several years as parents expressed continuing concerns about their children's isolation, unhappiness, and general lack of attachment within the school and neighborhood. Amerikaner and Omizo concluded that effective prescriptive intervention should include the parents.[1] While schools have traditionally addressed students' vulnerabilities, the needs of the parents have often been ignored, or, at best, they have been addressed by individual workshops or with each parent as a problem occurred. Just as a child may experience negative affect and feel separated from the mainstream of school life when placed in a special education class or program, parents may experience similar negative feelings. Providing an opportunity to listen and share positive and negative feelings, become engaged with others, and contribute to and benefit from the solutions of other parents served as the leaders' central goal for the parent support group.

Establishing a Parent Group

The director of pupil services brought together school social workers and learning disabilities teachers to discuss the feasibility of establishing parent support groups in each of the school district's four schools. While the school social workers were providing individual and group counseling to students, therapeutic support groups for parents were not a traditional function of support personnel in a school setting. The establishment of parent support groups was an innovative process going beyond the traditional role of the school's responsibility to the child.

The staff's first task was to decide if they could add this responsibility to their already-full schedule. The decision was affirmative. A myriad of questions ensued, including leadership; open or closed group; the length, frequency, and location of meetings; and ways to inform parents and obtain their participation. "Can I be an effective parent group leader?" was the unasked question. A medical social worker specializing in parent groups was employed to assist the staff in developing a model for a school-based parent support group.

The establishment of a parent support group involved three major facets: evening programs for parents jointly sponsored by the PTA and the Department of Pupil Services; an inservice/consultative program for the school's support staff, which became a microcosm of the dynamic interaction within the parent groups; and a series of four concurrent parent support groups, each led by a school social worker and learning disabilities teacher.

Planning for the Groups

The PTA program topics and personnel were chosen to complement the initiation of the parent groups and serve as an invitation to parents to join a group. Three learning-disabled young adults who had matriculated through the school's special education program and a director of a learning disabilities program for a local college formed the first panel. They spoke about the experience and feelings of being learning disabled, defined the criteria that separated successful from nonsuccessful learning-disabled college students (self-motivation and awareness/knowledge/acceptance of their learning disability), and addressed parents' concerns about what the future will hold for their children. One panelist emphatically stated, "When I was a sophomore, I finally told my mother that I did have a learning disability and she was just going to have to accept that fact." In his earlier comments, the panelist had said that his mother had repeatedly told him that none of her seven children could have any learning problems. The second panel was composed of an educational psychologist, a clinical psychologist, and a psychiatrist who described the diagnostic and prescriptive teaching, medication, and treatment issues for learning-disabled students. At each of these programs, announcements were made about the formation of parent discussion groups; handouts specifying the location, times, and co-leaders were also provided.

Concomitantly, with the PTA programs and the beginning of the four parent groups, the school social workers and learning disabilities teachers were participating in a series of four group consultation sessions. These meetings provided a model for the group leaders on the dynamics and process of group development. Staff questions initially centered on involving parents in a group. Personal letters were sent by the students' learning disabilities teacher. Later, each parent received a phone call from one of the co-leaders. Reactions encountered by the staff during the phone calls included ambivalence, anger, anxiety, and denial reminiscent of some parents' responses when they were first informed that their child might have a learning disability. The parents' anxiety heightened the staff's apprehension about leading a group. As these fears were shared with the consultant and colleagues, an understanding of the source of the parents' reactions developed and with it an increasing sense of comfort in becoming a group leader. What seem in retrospect to have been mundane questions, such as how to arrange the chairs, whether coffee and food should be available, and whether name tags should be used, were of major importance and suggested to the group leaders the difficulty of immediately focusing on feelings. Another concern of the staff was with being co-leaders: Could they work cooperatively and complement each other? Would they feel competitive? How would they handle their disagreements? How would each handle the parents' affect and request for information?

The Group Begins

Starting Up

As the parents arrived for the first meeting, they were invited to have coffee. Chairs were arranged in a circle. Following the co-leaders' introduction of themselves and a brief history of why the group was formed, parents were asked to introduce themselves and talk about how they felt when their child was first diagnosed as learning disabled. Comments ranged from a sense of relief that there was a reason for their child's problems to expressions of anger at the teachers, school, therapists, and other specialists, whose recommendations all seemed to differ. Some parents felt the label only confirmed what they already knew; for other parents it led to a discovery that they probably had a learning disability that had gone undetected when they were students. As the parents described their common experiences, there was a shared sense of excitement as issues began to emerge and be identified. Even though the parents wanted to stay on beyond the one-and-a-half hour session, the co-leaders closed the group with a summary of what they had heard and not heard, and a sense of the unexpressed needs and feelings of the group.

Middle Stages

In the second and third sessions, the framing questions dealt with what the parents thought about the previous session. Specific questions included: Should friends of a parent be allowed to attend? The answer was no. Should a session be taped for a member who could not attend? The group said yes, but the co-leaders felt that taping offered the potential for violation of confidentiality. After dealing with these questions, the primary worries of the parents emerged. Dependency and interdependency were driving issues. When and how should parents let go? When should a child be able to take responsibility for himself or herself? Parents also wanted answers to the following: How do we improve our child's academic skills and self-esteem? How much should we be involved with our child's teachers? What do we do about our child's frustration with homework? Anger at the professional educator for not coming through for their child and depression over their inability to help their child were common themes. One parent voiced for the group, "I feel guilty for not liking my child," while another tearfully spoke of her feelings of anguish and helplessness when her son told her, "I'm not good at anything." In these middle sessions, the parents began to deal with affective issues, and some parents were sufficiently secure to suggest that a fellow parent and child could benefit from psychotherapy.

Just as parents became aware of their feelings, the co-leaders had to recognize their countertransference feelings. Whether rescue fantasies are more prevalent among secondary-setting professionals would be an interesting study in that the co-leaders experienced, at some time, a strong need to assume the parents' responsibilities. Silence by the co-leaders became a powerful therapeutic tool for the parent group to assume its own direction and initiative. Countertransference around parenting issues and deciding what is appropriate to share from the leader's own background symbolized whether the leader would remain a leader or become a parent participant.

Ending the Group

Central to the support group process was handling separation in the concluding session. Separation themes had been a core issue to many parents in the group. The co-leaders responded by freeing the parents to identify their child's and then their own loneliness and isolation and gave them the oportunity for a new kind of interpersonal attachment. Rather than responding to the parents' emotional stress by "understanding" it, the leaders helped the parents to feel less powerless by providing them with an increased capacity for socially adaptive relationships. In this final session, several socially adaptive patterns emerged. First, the parents developed new and meaningful relationships with other parents. Using these new attachments, they were able to feel less isolated and to develop a network for self-support. Second, the parents were helped to use the group as a lever for obtaining increased socialization opportunities for their children in school and in the neighborhood. The courage to be their child's advocate empowered parents to feel less discouragement and helplessness. Plans were formulated to obtain information about the etiology of learning disabilities and to review brain research. The group developed plans for meeting with high school personnel to obtain information on the programs and services available to their children and offered to meet with parents of elementary school learning-disabled children to discuss and, perhaps, allay their fears about junior high school. Family group meetings were proposed as well as additional support groups for students. Third, the parents were given an opportunity to test their inner and outer communications within a new set of social relationships in a secure climate.

Looking Back

Lowry's observation that, "As caseworkers we really need four ears: one with which to listen to *what* is being said; one to attend to what is *not* being said; one to hear *how* it is being said; and one to heed the feelings *unexpressed,"* provided the therapeutic foundation for school-based parent support groups.[2] Within this framework, the co-leaders started with a concept that parents can be an effective and powerful source of mutual aid. Certain obstacles exist, as previously described, that interfere with the actualization of this goal. It became the goal of the co-leaders to help the parents identify these obstacles, become engaged and attached within the group, and contribute to and benefit from mutual problem solving. For the co-leaders, their capacity not to become defensive was critical, as the parents vilified the school's "best efforts" to serve their children. Parents' feelings of helplessness expressed as denigrating attacks on the school and its personnel were transformed through the group process into mutual and shared problem solving. The co-leaders accomplished this change by helping the parents understand that, as parents, they have the power to bring about significant and lasting changes for their children. The leaders offered the parents a means of handling problems by being a resource for them to communicate and clarify their concerns and transform the concerns into constructive activity designed to enhance their children's self-esteem.

Notes and References

1. M. Amerikaner and M. Omizo, "Family Interaction and Learning Disabilities," *Journal of Learning Disabilities,* 17 (1984), pp. 540–543.

2. F. Lowry "The Caseworker in Short Contact Services, *Social Work,* 2 (January 1957), p. 55. Emphasis in original.

From Hospital or Home to School: A Team Approach

Marilyn Sargon Brier

HAVING A CHILD WHO IS diagnosed with a life-threatening illness or a degenerative disease poses a variety of unique concerns for a family. The child who has a degenerative disease needs special education, and the family needs support. The fact that these children will not live to be adults means that their perspective on education will be different. The parents dealing with their child's life-threatening illness are faced with many stresses, including the effect of the illness on the total family and the daily realization that they are parenting a child who will not live to be an adult. Accompanying this anticipated loss of their child are their hopes and dreams for the future.

Pathways for Children, a three-year federally funded demonstration project, was established from a grant through the Handicapped Children's Early Education Program. It is a collaborative effort among various disciplines—social work, medicine, and education—to help families and children from birth through age 8 who have a life-threatening illness that interferes with the usual developmental and educational processes and leads to a shortened life span. This program is located in Canton, Massachusetts, at the Massachusetts Hospital School, a residential facility for physically handicapped children; it is the newest program administered by Enable, a nonprofit organization that provides medical, educational, and social services to handicapped people.

The main objectives of the Pathways for Children program are: (1) to maintain the child in the least restrictive educational environment for as long as possible; (2) to maintain the child's self-esteem despite the debilitating nature of the illness; and (3) to help the child and the family come to an understanding of death. For these goals to be achieved, appropriate support must be provided to each family and to the educators and other professionals involved with the family. This article focuses on describing the program, the staff roles, the program's educational component with a detailed explanation of the social worker's role, a case study to demonstrate social service interventions, and the importance of the interdisciplinary team.

The Pathways for Children Program

Pathways for Children consists of three components: direct service, indirect service, and model development and dissemination. Direct service refers to working with the child, the child's family, and other professionals involved with the child. Indirect service includes (1) providing workshops, presentations, and in-service training for educational and health care professionals and (2) lecturing to various groups and organizations to heighten public awareness about the needs of this population. Since Pathways for Children is a model program, it is mandated by the grant to document all the work done and to create a model that can be replicated nationally. Plans for the third year of operation include continuing to provide direct and indirect services and the dissemination of information about the program.

Staff Roles

The team consists of a program director, a social worker, a play therapist, a registered nurse, a secretary, and a special educator. At the initial intake, which occurs either in the hospital or at the patient's home, an overview of the services available is given, and consent forms and authorization forms for the release of medical and educational information are signed. It is at this time that the family's needs are determined and the appropriate team member is assigned.

The special educator is available to consult with school systems, develop workshops for teachers, and advocate for the child and his or her parents in the educational setting. The registered nurse is the liaison between the medical staff and the child and family. For example, a child in this program who has a rare genetic disease is seen twice a week by the nurse for feedings and walks and for collaborative observation with the developmental day care program staff. The nurse is then able to share with the child's primary physician any concerns she has or changes she has noticed in the child's health condition. The nurse may also support the family in caring for a child who is at home and needs medical care or treatments, for example, by providing physical therapy.

The play therapist is the advocate for the child's educational, medical, and emotional needs. If requested, she may accompany the child and the parents to medical procedures and treatments, providing them with emotional support. Through play therapy she is able to establish rapport with the child, helping the child to maintain a positive self-image and to develop an understanding of the disease or illness. She also encourages the child to express feelings and concerns and enables him or her to develop coping skills. While honoring the child's confidentiality, the play therapist is available to answer parents' questions regarding developmental issues and the child's coping ability.

Educational Component

An important part of Pathways for Children—one that makes this program unique—is the educational component. Because this component usually involves the team effort of the play therapist and social worker, its description will be followed by a case study and an explanation of the social worker's role. A main objective of the program is to provide children who have a life-threatening illness with an equal educational opportunity in the least restrictive environment for as long as possible. This goal is achieved through close working relationships with school systems, preschool programs, and early intervention teams to develop their awareness of their role in reaching out to the sick child and the family. Emphasis is placed on developing strong school liaisons with the school social worker, guidance counselor, or adjustment counselor to alleviate the child's isolation and make the transition easier from hospital or home to school. Staff support is also provided for the school nurse and classroom teacher through in-service programs and workshops.

Case Study

Having been hospitalized several times since school started in September because of his recent diagnosis of rhabdomyosarcoma (cancer of the soft tissue), 7-year-old Jason's school attendance was minimal. During one of his hospitalizations, a school meeting was arranged, attended by his classroom teacher; the school principal, nurse, and guidance counselor; the community visiting nurse (who had previously made one home visit); and the social worker, program director, and play therapist from Pathways for Children. At this meeting, staff representing Pathways for Children served as advocates for Mr. and Mrs. H and for Jason's educational needs, informing the school personnel of his medical condition and medical needs, while respecting Jason's medical confidentiality at the same time.

To facilitate the child's reentry into school and to make the transition easier for him, his classmates, and school personnel, Pathways for Children prepared the school regarding what to expect when he returned. Clearly, Jason's appearance and behavior would be different. These factors would affect his attitude toward returning to school. It was important to recognize that Jason, apprehensive from having been ill and hospitalized, was feeling a lack of control and a sense of powerlessness over his environment and his body. He was having to adjust to his new body image and changed appearance. Because he had had chemotherapy, his hair had fallen out; he had a wig, which he wore alternately with his baseball hat. Jason had also lost a lot of weight, was very pale, and had less stamina than previously.

Since he had missed so much school, he had limited contact with his peers and classmates and, in addition, he would feel behind in his schoolwork. Further outpatient treatments and clinic appointments might cause him to miss more school and to feel pressured to keep up with his classmates. Jason wanted to attend school, and his parents supported him. It was essential that he be able to attend school even if only for a short time each day, or whenever he felt well enough, because he needed the sense of normalcy and mastery that he would be able to achieve from school and his schoolwork. In addition, the anxiety and depression he was experiencing from being diagnosed as having a serious illness would be countered by his participating in the routine academic and social activities in school.[1] For the seriously ill child, "returning to school is vital because of the importance that school has in his or her life, the confirmation to the child that he or she is better, and the positive effect that mastery of stress has on future coping."[2]

The social worker explained to Jason's teacher the importance of treating him like any other child, allowing him to participate in regular classroom activities and encouraging him to work to his potential. The teacher's personal interest and encouragement would help Jason in his adjustment to returning to school and would also reflect how his classmates were to treat him. She would be pivotal in helping the other children to understand him and not be frightened by him. His teacher's positive attitude would also help his parents cope more positively with their feelings concerning their son's illness. For Jason to continue to find satisfaction and fulfillment in school would be of great importance to him and his parents.

The team also pointed out how Jason's return to school would be facilitated by preparing his classmates, their parents, and other teachers in the building for his return. In order to achieve a successful return to school, the team offered Jason's teacher support and help in this preparation, acting as a liaison between Jason and his parents and the school. The social worker suggested that his teacher discuss with Mrs. H ahead of time what and how much she felt comfortable having explained to Jason's classmates. When his teacher shared the concerns expressed by other teachers— "Jason shouldn't be in school because of the effect on the other children." "What about subjecting the other children to a child as sick as Jason?" "Is it fair for someone as sick as Jason to return to school?"— the Pathways for Children's team offered to help the staff examine some of their resistance and protective reactions along with their feelings of anxiety and discomfort. If school personnel are aware of their own reactions to serious illness and are able to understand how these reactions affect their decision-making ability concerning the seriously ill child, they will be better able to meet the needs of their students.[3]

A direction not yet realized by Pathways for Children, but planned for the future, includes workshops targeted for other community professionals and parents. The purpose of the workshops would be to examine and to discuss issues of death and dying, children's perceptions of death, and other concerns related to the seriously ill child and his or her world. For school personnel, the play therapist has compiled and edited "Death Education for Young Children: A Resource Guide for Educators," which includes a discussion of children's understanding of death at different developmental levels, based on literature and empirical information.[4] In-service training is also available to teachers, nurses, social workers, adjustment counselors, and guidance counselors about play therapy, physical limitations owing to illness, and clarification of medical needs. This training would also sensitize school personnel and educators to the special medical and emotional needs of seriously ill children.

Social Worker's Role

The responsibilities of the social worker in Pathways for Children focus around the family, with whom the social worker maintains communication. In the initial assessment of each family, an evaluation is made of (1) the family's knowledge, understanding, and acceptance of the child's condition; (2) the family's developmental expectations for the child; (3) the family's coping mechanisms for dealing with the terminal nature of the disease or illness; and (4) the communication patterns and relationships within the family —the family dynamics. The social worker offers support to individuals within the family or to the family as a unit. Although the social worker usually has more contact with the mother since she takes the child to treatments, stays with the child in the hospital, and is responsible for the child's overall care at home, it is advisable for the social worker to schedule evening or late afternoon visits to establish rapport also with the child's father and siblings. Forming a positive relationship with the family, especially the parents, is of great value in working with the family through the course of the child's illness and consequently during bereavement.

It has been important that the social worker be flexible and occasionally make unscheduled visits in order to provide support when needed, for example, when Jason, who was refusing to eat, needed to have a gastrostomy tube surgically inserted. When Jason's mother phoned the social worker to explain that he was having the surgery for the G-tube and that her husband was with her, the social worker arranged to make a brief visit to the hospital to initiate contact with the father and to provide support to both parents while they waited for Jason to have his surgery. In addition to direct intervention and assessment, the social worker's responsibilities include consulting with and acting as a liaison to other professionals and agencies.

Consultation

When the coordinator of volunteers from a hospice phoned the social worker to schedule a presentation on Pathways for Children, she requested that the social worker speak with one of her volunteers. This hospice volunteer was experiencing difficulty with one of her patients, a young child whose health was failing due to a cardiac problem and who was unable to share his fears and concerns. His parents, unable to cope with his deteriorating health and unable to encourage him to express his feelings with them, had taken him out of school for fear that exertion or excitement would cause cardiac arrest. Acting as a consultant, the social worker advised and made suggestions to the hospice volunteer and also sent her copies of bibliographies of helpful publications for parents and for children, compiled by the social worker and play therapist, respectively. In addition, feeling that Kubler-Ross's "The Dougy Letter" would encourage the child to give himself permission to express his feelings and growing fears, the social worker also sent a copy to the volunteer.[5] When the social worker and the play therapist later provided a program presentation to this hospice about Pathways for Children, support of the hospice volunteer was continued.

Community Liaison

In working with families, the social worker's responsibility is to use the existing resources in the communities and to coordinate both the educational and community resources. She is the liaison between the family and the community's resources. An example of just such networking concerns a family with eight children that had relocated from the Midwest to Massachusetts. Shortly before they moved, one of their children was diagnosed as having leukemia. This family needed support and help in obtaining housing. Having made many calls and researched the resources available, the social worker was able to help the family connect with real estate agents in the area, find them a school advocate from their new community for their special needs child, and connect them with an outreach support group. Through the networking and outreach facilitated by the social worker, this family is now settled in its new community, the children are attending school, and the child with leukemia is receiving treatments.

Bereavement

The social worker's support to the family continues as the child's medical condition deteriorates and the child dies. Following the child's death, families will still be followed, and support will be provided through the bereavement process. This support will be available through individual counseling or a bereavement group as long as families have the need. When appropriate, referrals will be made to Compassionate Friends, a self-help organization consisting of parents who have lost a child through various causes. Where necessary, the social worker will facilitate each family in making the transition to a bereavement group.

Another Aspect of the Case Study

The case study of Jason and his family illustrates the stress and strain affecting the family unit when a child becomes seriously ill, as with cancer. The whole family experiences the crisis of the diagnosis, and life will never be the same. Changes in family life, unexpected crises, and the fear of death necessitate direct intervention. Jason's parents, especially his mother, were having difficulty coping with their son's recent diagnosis, which had been unexpected and had caught them off-guard. All of a sudden, Mr. and Mrs. H's lives had been thrown into total confusion. "Their normal routines, relationships, roles, patterns of behavior, self-confidence, and sense of being in control of their own and their children's lives" were disturbed.[6] After a history of infertility, Mr. and Mrs. H adopted Jason, and later Elsie, who was now 2 years old. These children fulfilled their parents' hope of having a family. Now the future of her son and of her family group—that she had anticipated and worked so hard for—was unclear, frightening, and unpredictable. In addition, Mrs. H could no longer look forward to Jason's attending school each day with his neighborhood friends and being with his classmates. Instead, Mr. and Mrs. H had to take their son for regular visits to the hospital about thirty miles from their home, to be followed by surgery that required hospitalization. Child care had to be arranged for Elsie in order that Mr. H could visit Jason and Mrs. H could stay overnight with him. Jason's chemotherapy treatments resulted in hair loss and other physical changes that created additional stress and required further adjustment for each family member. Two-year-old Elsie was unable to understand where Jason was, why he wasn't home to play and fight with her, and why he seemed and looked different when he was at home.

According to Mrs H, before Jason became ill, he was a playful, outgoing child who reached out to others, played well by himself, and had many interests. Once hospitalized, he changed; he became withdrawn and irritable and refused to eat, drink, play, and care for himself. He showed no interest in his environment.

His depressed behavior, which was his reaction to his illness, increased his mother's frustration, fear, and anger. Not only was she overwhelmed by medical procedures and unfamiliar terminology, she was also feeling a lack of control over the medical process and both her life and her child's. She felt isolated and as though she were losing her independence, her parenting role, her very identity. Unable to deal with her feelings, she began to displace her anger onto the hospital, the doctors, and the nurses, blaming them for the poor care she thought her son was receiving. She also became very impatient and angry with Jason and, according to his physician, was unable to contain her anger or modify her behavior in front of her son. Having become engaged in a power struggle with his mother, Jason decided not to eat or drink and was very close to being in poor nutritional balance and in danger of death. Therefore, the medical staff felt they had to intervene, and the decision was made to insert the G-tube surgically. When Jason was finally discharged with Visiting Nurse follow-up, his mother was anxious and overwhelmed by all the care he required and the possibility of his suddenly having to be rushed back to the hospital at any time. Mrs. H also had to deal with Elsie's demands for attention and her anger at being left and ignored.

In working with Jason's family, the social worker focused on developing a trusting relationship with Mr. and Mrs. H so that they could feel safe and express their feelings of anger, helplessness, guilt, fear, and despair. She allowed them in a nonjudgmental way to work at their own pace, helping them cope at whichever stage they were in, be it denial, anger, bargaining, or depression. These stages or coping mechanisms, described by Kubler-Ross, are labels that help people identify some of the confusing feelings they have during stressful times.[7]

The social worker also discussed with Mr. and Mrs. H their expectations of Jason's treatment and encouraged them to examine how their attitudes affected Jason and Elsie. She also pointed out how Jason's understanding and acceptance of his illness was dependent on his parents and how they were dealing with him.[8] Along with helping Mrs. H accept her and her family's feelings, the social worker encouraged her to promote and enjoy the good family times they were able to share—to relish the moment and not to anticipate or project what was to come. Through frequent hospital visits, phone calls, and home visits, the social worker provided emotional support. Her efforts to maintain consistent family contact established the family's trust so that they could accept her help and realize that they were not alone.

In addition, the social worker tried to foster communication between Mr. and Mrs. H as a couple and also with the medical staff, with whom she encouraged them to articulate clearly their needs and concerns. She also advocated for Mr. and Mrs. H by interpreting and explaining to Jason's physician their behavior and reactions.

Resource Packets

Each team member has developed for the families a resource packet that contains a bibliography and other helpful information geared to different audiences. The social worker's packet contains a researched list of parent support groups in the various communities and information to help the family understand the illness. Her bibliography is for parents; it lists books on illness and death to enable parents to understand and explain to their children what is happening. The play therapist has prepared a bibliography for educators and another for children that lists books and stories about death grouped according to the child's chronological age. The nurse's bibliography contains books for community people.

Working on an Interdisciplinary Team

As a member of a team, the author of this article recognizes the importance of all the team members being able to work well together to ensure the success of the program and to serve best the families involved. The stages the team has experienced could well be described by the Lowe-Herranen Team Development Model.[9] This model suggests six stages: (1) becoming acquainted, (2) the trial and error stage, (3) collective indecision, (4) crises, (5) resolution, and (6) team maintenance.

The first stage, "becoming acquainted," affects how individuals enter the team. According to the model, "the method of entry is critical as it sets the tone for future interactions in terms of how the team functions within specific settings."[10] The Pathways for Children program director was hired first; then she interviewed and selected her team members, as mandated by the grant. Once the team was formed, its members started working at about the same time.

"The stage of 'trial and error' begins when there is an awareness of the need to work together toward a common goal of patient care."[11] Because they came from different backgrounds and disciplines, it was vital that the members understand the functions other professionals on the team would perform. This team has had to define and redefine its roles and specific expertise to avoid overlap and to develop a collegial, not competitive, working relationship.

The third stage, described as "collective indecision," occurs when the team tries to "avoid direct conflict and achieve an equilibrium."[12] The assumption is that responsibilities are shared and decisions are made by default. During this stage, the Pathways for Children team had difficulty making decisions owing to the members' desire to please one another. A vivid example of this indecision was the turmoil and frustration that the team experienced in trying to find a name for the program that the team members could agree upon. Team morale was low.

Faced with this indecision, the team entered the fourth stage, "crisis," during which time individual roles and responsibilities became more defined. Each member began to realize and recognize the other team members' knowledge and contributions to patient care.

The fifth stage, "resolution," was marked by the commitment to working together as a team. Through open communication— and shared leadership, decision-making, and responsibility sustained by team members' evaluation of their interactions—the team has been able to move on to the sixth stage, "team maintenance." This last stage is characterized by the team's sharing its understanding and recognizing its responsibilities as a team and as individuals.

Summary

October 1, 1984, started the second year of the three-year grant for Pathways for Children. After being in operation for more than a year, it became clear that certain aspects of the program required more time than initially anticipated. Community outreach efforts to increase public awareness and educate other professionals and agencies about Pathways for Children required an extensive amount of time and effort. Although the grant stated that forty families would be served in the first year, it wasn't until March 1984 that the first referral was received. As of December 1984, thirty-two families were being served. Outreach in the second year was ongoing, yet not as extensive as in the first year.

In view of the sensitive and emotionally-laden issues with which the program deals—the seriously ill child, his or her family, and death and dying—much stress is encountered. To prevent burnout and to deal effectively with the stress, it is necessary for team members "to assert control to avoid feeling helpless."[13] The team members of Pathways for Children deal with adapting to the stress by alternating the provision of direct care with tending to administrative responsibilities, that is, phone calls, presentations, and correspondence. Another method used is building in recreational and leisure-time activities individually or as a team. It is essential that there be ongoing support for staff and a safe, trusting forum created where emotionally laden issues can be discussed. The program addresses these issues by holding meetings with a consulting psychologist once a month for staff support and development.

A goal that Pathways for Children would like to achieve is that of creating both a support group for the parents of children in the program and a group for the children's siblings. Because the program covers a forty-mile radius around Canton, geographic location, distance, and transportation have interfered with forming a sibling group. In addition, the complex care required for some of the sick children, family responsibilities, and work schedules have made the formation of a parents' group difficult, although these groups are being considered by the author of this article.

Pathways for Children team members have found working with children who have a life-threatening illness or degenerative disease and with their families to be a privilege—and a highly rewarding one. To quote Koocher, the rewards of working with this group include "bringing physical or psychological comfort in times of pain or stress, helping to facilitate family life, and often accomplishing significant work with highly motivated patients in relatively short periods of time."[14] The resilience, strengths, and determination of the families and children involved in Pathways for Children are to be admired. There is much to be learned from them, not only about dying but also about living, because dying is a part of living.

Notes and References

1. N. U. Cairns et al., "School Attendance of Children with Cancer," *Journal of School Health,* 52, No. 3 (1982), p. 152.

2. J. W. Ross and S. A. Scarvalone, "Facilitating the Pediatric Cancer Patient's Return to School," *Social Work,* 27 (May 1982), p. 256.

3. D. Kaplan, A. Smith, and R. Grobstein, "School Management of the Seriously Ill Child," *Journal of School Health,* 44, No. 5 (1974), p. 250.

4. B. McNally, "Death Education for Young Children: A Resource Guide for Educators," development funded by Grant No. G00830224, U.S. Department of Education (Canton, Mass.: Pathways for Children, 1986).

5. E. Kubler-Ross, "The Dougy Letter," *A Letter to a Child with Cancer* (Escondido, Calif.: Shanti Nilaya, 1979).

6. This point about the parents of cancer patients was made in other articles. See J. W. Ross and H. Klar, "Mental Health Practice in a Physical Health Setting," *Social Casework*, 63 (1982), p. 148, citing E. H. Futterman and I. Hoffman, "Crisis and Adaptation in the Families of Fatally Ill Children," in J. Anthony and C. Koupernic, eds., *The Child in His Family, the Impact of Disease and Death*, Vol. 2 (New York: John Wiley & Sons, 1973).

7. E. Kubler-Ross, *On Death and Dying* (New York: Macmillan, 1969).

8. J. W. Ross, "Coping with Childhood Cancer: Group Intervention as an Aid to Parents in Crisis," *Social Work in Health Care*, 4, No. 4 (1979), p. 382.

9. J. I. Lowe and M. Herranen, "Understanding Teamwork: Another Look at the Concepts," *Social Work in Health Care*, 7, No. 2 (1981), p. 2.

10. Ibid., p. 2.

11. Ibid., p. 3.

12. Ibid., p. 3.

13. G. P. Koocher, "Adjustment and Coping Strategies among the Caretakers of Cancer Patients," *Social Work in Health Care*, 5, No. 2 (1979), p. 148.

14. Ibid., p. 141.

Benefits of Early Intervention to Prevent Truancy

Renee Shai Levine

AT NATIONAL AND STATE LEVELS, reports concerned with reversing the rising tide of mediocrity in public education have called attention to revising the criteria for curriculum and teacher competency. Recognition has also been given to the support that attendance and parent participation provide in achieving goals for excellence in education [1]

Professionals responsible for developing plans for children are aware that nonattendance is a symptom of unresolved problems that may reside within the child, the home, the school, or the community. [2] A review of earlier studies establishes that these factors are present early in the child's school career and are easier to arrest or redirect successfully when intervention occurs early in the child's school experience. [3] The concern for the plight of truants is not limited to administrators, teachers, and pupil personnel in the schools—it extends to social workers in public and voluntary child welfare agencies. The Juvenile Justice and Delinquency Prevention Act of 1974 provided the sanction for furthering state efforts to remove truants from the category of "delinquents" to that of "deprived" children. They were removed from the jurisdiction of the courts and placed under the care of the child welfare agencies. [4]

The traditional disease model of prevention involves isolating and treating a causal agent as a means of eradicating the problem. In this model, the distinctive patterns of particular diseases are studied to determine the natural history of the disease and the locus of its origins.[5] The early models for the prevention of public health and social problems accept that there are multiple causal factors in the environment of the population at risk and that the services needed to treat these problems require the collaboration of various types of organizations.[6] More recent models include the expectation that target groups can learn the behaviors needed to overcome causal factors contributing to the problem.[7] Models attempting to address the multiple factors contributing to public health and social problems also accept the fact that preventive intervention may occur prior to the occurrence of a visible need.[8] Knowing the sources or causes of the problem to be treated is a necessary prerequisite to determining the preventive model for each particular problem at issue.[9]

Truancy has been identified as a problem that contributes to the incidence of vandalism and delinquency in the community as well as to a lack of continuity of learning for those out of school and those in the classroom.[10] Those out of school are not learning. Children who attend are held back when teachers must review work for those who have been absent.[11]

Two key factors in disincentives for attendance have been poor grades and retention in grade.[12] Other important factors are poor interpersonal skills accompanied by low self-esteem and lack of self-confidence.[13] Key factors in enforcing school attendance have been parental knowledge and involvement.[14] There has been considerable documentation that unless the parent is involved and reinforces the expectations for school attendance, the school's efforts with the child will be seriously blocked.[15] Teacher absence has also been found to be a factor contributing to truancy.[16] Levine used these findings to develop a tool to identify those factors that may be presenting barriers to attendance for particular children.[17]

This article will report the findings of a pilot project done in a Philadelphia, Pennsylvania, elementary school to provide data to answer these questions:

1. To what extent are the factors known to contribute to truancy discernible in the early grades?

2. How will parents respond to the school's outreach for closer home and school collaboration in behalf of their child?

3. In what ways does the outreach benefit the child?

4. What are other outcomes of the home and school collaboration?

Methodology

The school in which the pilot project occurred was located in a white, working-class community. The students in the project were from this community. The project was developed in close cooperation with the school principal, school counselor, and teachers. The second grade was selected as the target group because the school had prior recorded experiences with these children. The critical incidence of absence was defined as eighteen days during the previous school year. Those second-grade children who had been absent eighteen days or more during the first grade had missed 10 percent of the school year and were presumed to be vulnerable, whether or not the absence was excused. The children in this category were referred to as Group A. Children absent seventeen days or less were referred to as Group B.

Levine's tool was used to guide the identification of children having factors known to contribute to truancy. (See Table 1.) The

Table 1.
Assessment Tool for Early Intervention in the Prevention of Truancy

I. The Child	II. The Home	III. The School	IV. The Community
A. School phobia	A. Parental knowledge[c]	A. Adequate reporting, recording, and follow-up	A. Peer influence
B. Interpersonal skills	B. Family attitude[d]	B. Inconsistent enforcement	B. Street gangs
C. Ethnic or racial dissonance	C. Family socio economic status	C. Relevance of curriculum	C. Interracial tensions
D. Failure to learn[a]	D. Family situation	D. Appropriate school placement	
E. Learning style[a]	E. Child abuse or neglect	E. Retention and promotion	
F. Learning disabilities[b]	F. Parenting skills	F. School transitions[a]	
G. Health problems		G. Suspension and expulsion	
		H. Competent, concerned teachers	
		I. Teacher absenteeism	
		J. School environment	

SOURCE: R. S. Levine, "An Assessment Tool for Early Intervention in Cases of Truancy," *Social Work in Education*, 6 (Spring 1984), p. 136.
[a]Affected by III-C, III-D, and III-E.   [b]Affected by III-C and III-D.
[c]Affected by III-A.   [d]Affected by III-B.   [e]Affected by IV-B and IV-C.

cumulative school records of the second-grade children were reviewed to determine if the factors were discernible. These records included data about the sex and age of a child, whether or not the child had been retained in a grade or had attended kindergarten, and the number of residential and school changes experienced since entering school. Of the sixty-nine children registered in second grade on October 3, 1983, cumulative records were available for sixty-six. Of these, 28.8 percent (nineteen) were found to have had absences equal to or more than eighteen days in the first grade. Their teachers were contacted to introduce the researcher and the project. The teachers were interviewed for their perceptions and concerns about these children in the classroom. Data gathered from these interviews were included in the preparations for parent interviews. The school counselor and school nurse were also asked to share any concerns or problems they may have had about the children in the target group.

Parent interviews began November 10, 1983, and were conducted until February 13, 1984. Interviews were arranged by telephone, by messages left with neighbors, or by mail. Of the nineteen families, 21 percent (four) had disconnected their phones. Another 21 percent (four) did not have phones in their homes. Despite these barriers, interviews were held with parents of sixteen of the nineteen children. Fifteen of the parents signed consent slips to participate in the project. Eight of the interviews took place in the home, and eight took place in school. Three parents never responded to the request for an interview. Follow-up interviews were held at the end of the school year. Children who were being reviewed for special education placement were not included in the project. One child who was absent seventeen days, but was at risk of failing, was included in the project.

The preliminary findings from the interviews with teachers and parents led to the formation of a small-group activity for boys. The group met at lunchtime on Mondays from mid-December until the last week of school in June 1984. The program consisted of low-skill, high-return, craft activities and was organized for the purpose of fostering the self-esteem, confidence, and interpersonal skills of the children selected to participate.

The school district's form for teacher attendance was used to determine the extent of a teacher's absence the previous year. Those teachers who had exhausted their sick leave and personal leave days and had additional absence were considered to have excessive absence. In this school district, teachers were allotted ten days sick leave per school year, three personal leave days, and leaves for a variety of family and personal reasons. For the purposes of this study, a teacher who had been absent fourteen days or more was considered to have had excessive absences. The data collected from the cumulative school records, the interviews with teachers and parents, the small-group sessions with the boys, and the school district's form for teacher attendance contributed to the findings reported.

Findings

Factors Contributing to Truancy Discernible in the Early Grades
    A major finding of the project was that the factors known to contribute to truancy enumerated in Levine's tool are discernible in the early grades. The cumulative school records were found to provide a rich source of data in identifying these factors.[18]
Sex.   In earlier reports describing children who are truant, the data indicated that there were a larger number of boys than girls in this group.[19] Although the number of boys in Group A was greater than the number of girls, the association between sex and attendance was not found to be significant when measured by chi square. Sex was found to be related to vulnerability in identifying those who were retained in grade, by attendance. (See Table 2.)
Age.   Age was not found to be a factor contributing to vulnerability for the children in this sample. The age span of

Table 2.
Factors Contributing to Truancy Discernible in the First-Grade Cumulative School Records, by Number and Percentage

Factors	All (N=66)				Group A (n=19)[a]				Group B (n=47)[b]			
	Male		Female		Male		Female		Male		Female	
	n	%	n	%	n	%	n	%	n	%	n	%
Sex	34	51.5	32	48.5	11	57	8	43	23	49	24	51
Retention in Grade by Sex	11	68.7	5	31.3	5	83	1	17	6	60	4	40

    [a]Absent 18 days or more (includes one child absent 17 days, who was at risk for failing).
    [b]Absent 17 days or less.

Table 3.
Factors Contributing to Truancy Discernible in the First-Grade Cumulative School Records, by Number and Percentage

Factors	All (N = 66)		Group A (n = 19)[a]		Group B (n = 47)[b]	
	n	%	n	%	n	%
Retention in grade	16	24.0	6	31.5	10	21.0
No kindergarten attendance	16	24.0	7	36.8	9	19.0
Residential changes	19	28.0	6	31.5	13	27.7
School changes	13	19.6	4	21.0	9	19.0
Teacher with excessive absence	19	28.6	6	31.5	13	27.7

[a]Absent 18 days or more (includes one child absent 17 days, who was at risk for failing).

[b]Absent 17 days or less.

children in the entire group and in Group A both varied by 2 years 2 months between the oldest and youngest. The age span of children in Group B was 1 year 10 months. The difference was not significant.

Retention in Grade. The children who had been absent eighteen days or more (Group A) were found to be more likely to have been retained in grade than those who had not. The grade most often repeated was first grade. Fifteen percent (ten) of those retained had been retained in first grade, 4.5 percent (three) in kindergarten, and 4.5 percent (three) in second grade. (See Table 3.) When those who had been retained in grade by sex were examined, the data supported the fact that boys are more vulnerable than girls. (See Table 2.)

No Kindergarten Attendance. Kindergarten attendance was found to be a critical variable for children who had been absent eighteen days or more in first grade. Nearly twice as high a percentage of the children in Group A (36.8 percent) were found not to have attended kindergarten compared to those in Group B (19 percent). (See Table 3.) Attendance in kindergarten was seen as important in assisting children to develop those skills needed for progress in school and for positive attendance patterns.

Residential Changes. The number of residential changes a family had had since the child registered in school was yet another factor discerned to be present more often in the experience of children who had been absent eighteen days or more. It was a reflection of marital break-up and/or changing economic circumstances and can be viewed as an indicator of greater vulnerability. (See Table 3.) *School Changes.*   Another factor found to contribute to truancy discernible in the early grades was school changes. Those absent eighteen days or more in the first grade were found to have been more likely to have attended more than one school than those absent seventeen days or less. This factor was found to be related to both the child's attendance and progress in learning. We found that 75 percent of the children in Group A who had attended more than one school were retained in a grade compared to 30 percent of those in Group B. (See Table 3.)

School changes in this sample often represented transfers in and out of Catholic schools. The reasons for the transfers were economic stress in the family or children's performance in school. Thus, school change can be a factor that serves as a symptom of problems that contribute to school absence.

Teacher Absence.   Another factor found to contribute to truancy and discernible in the early grades was teacher absenteeism. The inability to predict how long a teacher would be out often resulted in a sequence of substitutes being assigned to a particular class room. The findings indicated that a higher percentage of children with excessive absence had a teacher with excessive absence than did those children with better attendance. (See Table 3.) In addition to the problem teacher absence presented for educational continuity, it was found to contribute to the unreliable recording of testing and attendance data.

Teachers' Perceptions.   The data from the interviews with teachers indicated that attendance alone was not an indicator of how well a child performed in the classroom. Almost half of the children in Group A did well in school work. There were 47.3 percent (nine) who were reported as working well at mastering their math and reading skills, 15 percent (three) who were trying hard but could not do the work, and 21 percent (four) who were doing poorly. There was also a range of behaviors in the children in this group. Only 21 percent (four) of these children were described as being able to get along with others and as good workers. (See Table 4.)

Parental Responses to School Outreach

The responses of parents (n = sixteen) in this sample to the opportunity to have a closer working relationship with the school

Table 4.
Teachers' Perceptions of the Characteristics of Children in Group A, by Number and Percentage ($n = 19$)

Teachers' Perceptions	n	%
Works well at mastering math and reading skills	9	47.3
Tries hard, but cannot do work	3	15.0
Does poorly in mastering math and reading skills	4	21.0
Gets along well with others and has good work habits	4	21.0
Poor concentration and work habits	11	57.8
Poor interpersonal skills	8	41.1
Poor self-concept	4	21.0

in the interests of their children were found to fall into two categories:

1. The parents who collaborated were found to fall into two groups.

   a. Some parents (n = six, or 37.5 percent) had concerns about the progress their children were making in mastering skills in math and reading, behavior, or interpersonal relationships. They freely shared their family situations and their concerns about their children, and they cooperated to work out a plan.

   b. Other parents (n = four, or 25.0 percent) denied that the child in the second grade was having a problem or needed extra attention but were interested in using the contact to raise concerns about an older sibling. (These four parents were also counted in category 2b below, making total percentages exceed 100.0.)

2. The parents who did not collaborate were also found to fall into two groups.

   a. Some parents (n = five, or 31.2 percent) had children who, despite poor attendance, were doing very well in the classroom. They saw no need for collaboration.

   b. Other parents (n = five, or 31.2 percent) denied that the children needed help outside the home. These parents wanted to feel that all that was needed was being done in their homes.

A review of the data from the interviews with parents indicated that children from families in categories 1a and 2a were from intact homes with two parents and from single-parent households, with parents who were either employed or unemployed, and with parents who had and had not completed high school. The parents in these categories proved to be feisty, well-organized people.

The children whose parents fell into category 1b were all from two-parent families where parents were employed and might also be in category 2b. The parents in category 2b were in the same demographic groups as those in 1a and 2a but proved to be people with histories of mental and medical illness. These parents expended a great deal of energy dealing with their own crises and found the demand to cope with the special needs of their children to be overwhelming. Their children tended to be seen by the teachers as "immature." In 75 percent of the instances of parents in category 1b (three out of four cases), the children demanding the attention of the parents were in the special education program. A child who had acting-out behavior and was felt to have emotional problems by the home and the school represented the remaining 25 percent.

The findings in the parent responses revealed that in instances where parents did indicate a need for resources to improve the child's achievement or behavior, services were not always readily available in the community or in the school. Of the parents who did agree to participate in the effort to have the home and school work closer together in behalf of the child's interest, 18.7 percent (three) were referred to a community resource, 12.5 percent (two) were referred to an existing school program, and 37.5 percent (six) were referred to the small-group activity created as part of this program.

Other findings demonstrated that, although the parents were concerned about their child's well-being and progress in school, the multiple factors creating stress in their own lives made it difficult for all to use their initiative in reaching out and arranging for the resources to support the child's progress. Parents did cooperate when the school was willing to develop a resource. Fifty-six percent (nine) of the parents were referred to resources in the school or community; 44 percent (seven) used them. Thirty-seven and a half percent (six) were parents whose children participated in the in-school group activity created as part of the program. (The parents of the two students referred to existing school programs were not counted in this group, because the author did not have responsibility for working directly with them.) Having a school-based stigma-free program made it possible for children to receive help when parents were unable or unwilling to collaborate in working with community agencies. The service most used by parents was the one based in the school.

The Group Program

Another major finding was that the outreach effort did assist in the identification and development of supports to maximize the child's growth. The outreach to the parents showed that in many instances parents were unable to collaborate with the school to develop supports for their children because of the multiple unresolved problems they faced in their personal health and life situations. Recognizing that the problems common to most of the children who were absent eighteen days or more (Group A) were poor interpersonal skills and low self-confidence and that the community did not provide resources to meet these needs, a small-group activity with this purpose was organized during the lunch hour. The group program was found to be effective in:

- changing the quality of the classroom interaction of the group participants;
- enhancing the professional behavior of the school personnel with the child and parents; and
- stimulating positive recognition for the child in the home.

The activity also provided an opportunity for an informal, productive, and personally rewarding experience as part of the school day.

Being able to participate in the group provided these children (all boys) an opportunity to experience themselves as having something special. They were excused from the lunchroom to eat in a small room with just a few others. Lunch was followed by a creative craft project using materials they enjoyed working with to complete a desirable project successfully. An interesting finding was that regardless of their behavior in the classroom and the chastisement some had to experience from their teachers, the boys' first concern in completing a project was whether they could show it to their teacher. These children were desirous of approval. The teachers were supportive in that they not only rewarded the boys with their approval, but they allowed them the opportunity to use their work in making a positive contribution to the class program.

The findings support the observation that the group was not

perceived as a program for children with problems. The feelings of being special projected by the group members and the projects shared in the classroom resulted in their classmates seeking out the worker to inquire, "What do I have to do to join?" Although the children participating in the group had low self-confidence and poor work habits, during the group sessions they behaved appropriately and were productive. The discussions that arose during this activity program suggested that they could also benefit from participation in a problem-solving group.

Changing Classroom Interaction.   The teachers reported that participation in the group served to change the attitudes of the children toward school and reduced the alienation and isolation of these children from their peers. One child who had a tendency to oversleep and to come after lunch on Mondays startled the teacher when he came rushing in, although late, on Monday mornings. She was convinced that this change was related to an interest in being in school for the Monday group meetings. Another teacher reported that her awareness of the program made her more sensitive to one child's good points; the mother of this child noticed that the teacher's notes complaining of his behavior stopped when he became part of the group.

Enhancing Professional Behavior.   The teachers used the insights from the group participation and the family situations to develop purposeful patterns to help children learn. They provided recognition for the work the children were doing in the group. They developed techniques that fostered paying attention and that were nonthreatening. One teacher developed a reward system to encourage positive participation in the classroom. This was particularly effective for children seeking positive approval.

The principal, too, found that having the program contributed to the enhancement of her professional role. Because of the child's involvement in the group, a parent of a boy who was seriously disturbed was helped to become involved with a psychiatric program in the community. The principal was aware of the problems the mother was having with the child and the burdens she was carrying in her own life. When the child was reported for acting-out behavior, the principal used her discretion and handled the situation within the school. She recognized that the parent was engaged in getting the help that was needed and would not benefit from the additional stress created by the reporting of an additional instance of inappropriate behavior.

Positive Recognition in the Home.   The rewards for the child's productive group activity created ripple effects that were felt in the home. The evident pleasure exhibited by some parents when the children brought their projects home resulted in desired approval and praise. This was further enhanced when the parents proudly shared the projects with neighbors and friends. In another instance, an activity project served as a link between a second grader and his high school brother. The craft became a resource for the brother's high school assignment. The data indicated that an unanticipated benefit of the program was the "spin-off" of attention and approval the child received in the home.

Other Outcomes of Home and School Collaboration

The findings also demonstrated the relationship of parental response to the opportunity for home and school collaboration and the child's performance in school. An examination of the results of the children's level of achievement in math and reading skills and the teacher's perceptions of their behaviors and interpersonal skills revealed that two-thirds (four) of the children whose parents were in category 1a (children needed help and parents collaborated) met the expectations to master their math and reading skills at the expected level for their grade, or above. The two children whose work was below grade level were seen as improving. One was being seen in a community clinic and was getting the emotional and educational supports to overcome his barriers to learning. The other was an immigrant child whose parents were making efforts to collaborate with school personnel to reinforce the child's developing of disciplined study habits. Two-thirds (four) of this group (all boys) took part in the group activity and one-third (two) took part in the project on an individual basis. These boys were all reported to have improved in developing self-esteem and interpersonal relations.

Of the children whose parental responses fell into category 1b (concern with an older sibling), 50 percent (two) were retained in grade and 50 percent (two) made strong gains in mastering the expectations for math and reading skills. The findings for the children whose parental responses were in category 2a (the child was doing well and parents did not need to become involved) revealed that the parents had made accurate assessments of the child's ability to succeed in meeting the school's expectations for learning. All these children achieved at the expectation for the grade or above and tended to be independent, self-motivated learners.

Those children whose parental responses fell into category 2b (the children had problems that the parents denied) did not make adequate progress in their learning. Sixty percent (three) were retained in grade. The 40 percent who participated in the group activity were reported to have changed their attitude toward school and moved from being isolated to having interpersonal exchanges with other children. The lack of parental cooperation in arranging other community services resulted in inadequate mastery of math and reading skills.

Conclusion

The outcomes of the pilot project confirm that early intervention to prevent truancy benefit the child in the home and in school. The factors contributing to truancy enumerated in Levine's tool are discernible in the early grades and can be used to develop programs for outreach to parents in behalf of the interests of their children.[20] The composite profile of the child who is most vulnerable was found to be a boy who has not attended kindergarten, has been absent eighteen days or more in first grade, has been retained in first grade, lives in a family with parents who have mental or physical illness, has had one or more residential or school changes since he registered in school, and has a teacher with a record of excessive absence. If the factors creating barriers to learning and attendance are to be reduced or overcome, they require attention from both the home and the school.

Some of the factors exist prior to the child's enrollment in school, and others occur while the child is in school. Some are rooted in circumstances over which neither the family nor the school have control. Others are located in the practices and policies of the family and the school. The purpose of explicating the causal factors is not to cast blame but to indicate the benefits to be derived from collaboration between home and school.

The project also demonstrates that early intervention benefits the school. It becomes a vehicle for establishing school accountability to reduce and overcome barriers to learning and attendance. In those instances where the school reaches out to engage parents in behalf of their children, the rejection of help and denial of a problem result in the failure to seek the very services needed for educational gains. The identification of this outcome is a support for those personnel whose function it is to assist parents who are overwhelmed with life's pressures to affirm their responsibility to their child's needs.

In addition, the project demonstrates that the school has the data—that is, the cumulative school records and school district's form for teacher attendance—needed to identify the children who can benefit from early intervention. It has the data needed to develop purposeful intervention for prevention with both children and teachers. In some cases, the prior knowledge of planned extended teacher absence can permit long-term teacher assignments to ensure educational continuity and accurate maintenance of records. The benefits of early intervention support the professional functions of the classroom teacher and of the principal with the child's parents, making the educators' behavior more purposeful and less personal.

The use of the school for early intervention provides benefits for parents. The school site provides an opportunity for identification of those factors creating barriers to learning and attendance. It also provides a site for services parents can use with comfort. School services are seen as supports for children that do not incur the stigma associated with other community resources.

It is important to provide services while children are young and it is still possible to work on overcoming problems of poor concentration, poor work habits, and low self-esteem. Efforts to reduce these problems require purposeful programs. If left unattended, they become the source of failure in school work and in interpersonal relationships. They contribute to the number of children who are truant and become unemployable.

The pilot project demonstrates that the use of a trained social work professional whose function is to foster home and school collaboration contributes to the identification of problems to be overcome and to the development of creative alternative solutions. Social workers in community agencies or in the schools can assist school administrators in developing projects to reduce barriers to learning and attendance. Other issues to be studied include all of the following:

- The extent to which the early involvement of parents on the school team will promote children's school attendance.

- The extent to which the ethnicity and socioeconomic class of the parents are factors in their involvement on the school team.

- The extent to which policies for teachers' absences can be developed to consider the learning needs of children.

- The extent to which families with children at risk can be identified through an analysis of existing public service systems—that is, child protective services, mental health and mental retardation, and public assistance—in the community.

Notes and References

1. See U.S. Department of Education, *A Nation at Risk: The Imperative for Educational Reform* (Washington, D.C.: U.S. Government Printing Office, 1983). See also, D. Thornburgh, *Turning the Tide: An Agenda for Excellence in Pennsylvania Public Schools* (Harrisburg: Commonwealth of Pennsylvania, October 1983).

2. D. Acker and B. J. Stembridge, "Pupil Personnel Workers as Change Agents in the Reduction of Truancy among Inner City Students," *Journal of the International Association of Pupil Personnel Workers*, 21 (March 1977), pp. 80–85, and 24 (March 1980), pp. 113–120.

3. L. N. Robins and E. Wish, "Childhood Deviance as a Developmental Process: A Study of 223 Urban Black Men from Birth to 18," in M. Bloom, ed., *Life Span Development: Bases for Preventative and Interventive Helping* (New York: Macmillan Publishing Co., 1980).

4. M. P. Thomas, "Status Offenders and Public Schools," *School Law Bulletin*, 9 (July 1978), p. 5. Cf. J. T. Johnson, "A Truancy Program: The Child Welfare Agency and the School," *Child Welfare*, 55 (September–October 1976), pp. 573–580.

5. M. Bloom, *Primary Prevention: The Possible Science* (Englewood Cliffs, N.J.: Prentice-Hall, 1981), pp. 9–11.

6. J. S. Mausner and A. K. Bahn, *Epidemiology: An Introductory Text* (Philadelphia: W. B. Saunders, 1974), cited in Bloom, *Primary Prevention*, p. 11.

7. Bloom, *Primary Prevention*.

8. Ibid, pp. 13–14.

9. Ibid, p. 12.

10. B. Demsch and J. Garth, "Truancy Prevention: A First Step in Curtailing Proneness," *Journal of the International Association of Pupil Personnel Workers*, 15 (June 1971), pp. 119–129.

11. G. W. Teachman, "In-School Truancy in Urban Schools: The Problem and a Solution," *Phi Delta Kappan*, 61 (November 1979), pp. 203–205.

12. See D. Schreiber, "School Dropouts," *National Education Association Journal*, 51 (May 1962), p. 52; and J. Snee, "The School Dropouts: The Why of Leaving," *Journal of the International Association of Pupil Personnel Workers*, 17 (March 1973), pp. 103–105.

13. A. Nielsen and D. Gerber, "Psychosocial Aspects of Truancy in Early Adolescence," *Adolescence*, 14 (Summer 1979), pp. 313–326. See also, M. Fine and C. Brownstein, "Parent Education and the School Social Worker," *Social*

Work in Education, 6 (Fall 1983), pp. 44–45; and G. A. Goff and G. D. Demetral, "A Home-Based Program to Eliminate Aggression in the Classroom," *Social Work in Education*, 6 (Fall 1983), pp. 5–14.

14. R. Miles and H. R. Ury, "A Study of Families in Need of Restoration," *Journal of the International Association of Pupil Personnel Workers*, 22 (March 1978), pp. 78–84; S. Birdsong, "Truancy: A Review of the Literature," *Journal of the International Association of Pupil Personnel Workers*, 24 (March 1980), p. 123; "Attendance: The Bottom Line," *NASSP Bulletin*, 63 (February 1979), pp. 32–38; and S. A. Saltsman, "School Attendance in the State of Maryland," *Journal of the International Association of Pupil Personnel Workers*, 24 (January 1980), pp. 49–52.

15. See J. O. Potthoff, "Late Again? Three Techniques to Reduce Tardiness in Secondary Learning Handicapped Students," *Teaching Exceptional Children*, 11 (Summer 1979), pp. 146–148; V. J. Stenson, "Crisis Theory: A United Approach to Truancy," *Journal of the International Association of Pupil Personnel Workers*, 24 (January 1980), pp. 54–62; J. Shelton and M. Garrett, "An Evaluation of the Use of Court Action Against Parents in Attendance Cases," *Journal of the International Association of Pupil Personnel Workers*, 21 (January 1977), pp. 44–49; F. Poole, "The School's Professional Responsibility for Casework to Parents," *Child Welfare*, 38 (June 1959), pp. 24–27; Demsch and Garth, "Truancy Prevention"; R. N. Suprina, "Cutting Down on Student Cutting," *NASSP Bulletin*, 63 (February 1979), pp. 27–31; and Miles and Ury, "A Study of Families in Need of Restoration."

16. P. G. Elliott, "Where Are the Students and Teacher? Student and Teacher Absenteeism in Secondary Schools," *Viewpoints in Teaching and Learning*, 55 (Spring 1979), pp. 19 and 23–24. See also C. Bamber, *Student and Teacher Absenteeism* (Bloomington, Ind.: Phi Delta Kappa Educational Foundation, 1979).

17. R. S. Levine, "An Assessment Tool for Early Intervention in Cases of Truancy," *Social Work in Education*, 6 (Spring 1984), pp. 133–150.

18. Ibid.

19. L. M. Daniels and A. A. Robinson, "Project Hold: A Way to Hold Them," *Negro Educational Review*, 30 (October 1979), p. 258; M. B. Katz and I. E. Dancy, "School Attendance and Early Industrialization in a Canadian City: A Multivariable Analysis," *History of Education Quarterly*, 18 (Fall 1978), p. 274; R. S. Neil and L. De Bruler, "The Effects of Self-Management of School Attendance by Problem Adolescents," *Adolescence*, 14 (Spring 1978), p. 177; and Nielsen and Gerber, "Psychosocial Aspects of Truancy in Early Adolescence," p. 316.

20. Levine, "An Assessment Tool for Early Intervention in Cases of Truancy."

A Last Resort: Truancy Referrals to Juvenile Court

Nancy Kramer Banchy

THERE IS A LIVELY DEBATE regarding appropriate truancy intervention. Much of the debate centers on whether status offenses such as truancy should be removed from the jurisdiction of the juvenile court. Some argue that the responsibility for truancy lies solely with the school. This article describes one city's effort to grapple with the issue and to design a continuum of interventions that relies on the resources of both the school and the juvenile court. The discussion includes exigencies that precipitated the truancy pilot project: a shared belief that truancy is a "signal for attention," and, if left unattended, a precursor of more serious problems; a 1983–84 truancy study of court interventions and their impact on school attendance; and a compilation of school district truancy statistics, including characteristics of students truant during the same period. Implications for school social work practice are reviewed, with emphasis on the need for continued work with chronically truant students and their families, and on the desirability of viewing the juvenile court as an intervention of last resort.

Background Information

Hennepin County Juvenile Court in Minneapolis, Minnesota, serves the school districts of Minneapolis and surrounding suburbs. The Minneapolis Public Schools (MPS), with a 1983–84 student population of 37,339, is the largest district within the county and includes most of the county's minority population. The district has a long history of providing social services to achieve educational goals. Truant officers first were employed early in the twentieth century. With the merging of visiting teachers in 1917, the district acquired one of the first school social work departments in the nation. Social workers currently are assigned to all schools, and they share attendance and truancy responsibilities as members of multidisciplinary teams.

Historically, the district has recognized the complexity of truant behavior. This view has been corroborated in the literature. Johnson stressed that truancy very often is a symptom of school, family, psychological, or social problems. She identified four major problem groupings: (1) disconnection from the school, (2) family difficulties, (3) emotional disturbances, and (4) peer pressure.[1] Levine developed an assessment tool citing multiple factors that have been documented in the literature as influencing truancy. Factors are identified in four major sectors: the child, the home, the school, and the community.[2]

The district has sought assistance from the juvenile court in remediating truant behavior. In Minnesota, although removed from the definition of "delinquent child," students of compulsory school age (7 to 15 years old) who are habitually truant may be referred to court. Since truancy is defined as a status offense, dispositional alternatives for adjudicated truants are limited by statute. The Hennepin County Juvenile Court, however, has allocated resources for truancy interventions based on research, expertise, and experience showing that delinquency often begins with truancy.

In identifying "red flags" that indicate the need for intervention with troubled youths, Compton noted "a sudden drop in achievement coupled with truancy."[3] Mauser reported that "one of the most frequently cited behavioral manifestations found in the literature related to juvenile delinquency has been truancy."[4] Miller and Windhauser delineated the following sequence for delinquency-prone students: reading retardation throughout primary and intermediate grades; gradual truancy in secondary grades because students cannot legally leave school; delinquency as an outlet to find "success" unobtainable in school.[5] In 1974 the U.S. Department of Health, Education, and Welfare also reported that although there is not necessarily a link between educational disability and delinquency, there is a common triad of reading problems, truancy, and delinquency.[6] Presiding Hennepin County Juvenile Court Judge

Allen Oleisky stated his belief that working with young truant students may prevent them from reappearing in the courts later. He cited a Hennepin County survey done in the mid-1970s indicating that approximately 95 percent of juveniles who are treated as adults after committing serious crimes had their first contact with the courts as truants.[7]

Because of these shared beliefs, school and court cooperation in truancy has been ongoing for years. Subsequent events, however, created a need for reevaluation. Minnesota law was changed in 1982 to simplify the process of truancy court referral from petition to citation and to define truancy as seven unexcused full day absences, or, for secondary students, seven hours on seven days.

Concomitantly, in 1982 MPS embarked on a comprehensive long-range planning process. The "Five-Year Plan" focused on achieving equity and excellence in education for all students and accountability based on learner outcomes. Social promotion was abolished, and benchmark tests at various grade levels were initiated. All evaluation data demonstrated the close link between school achievement and attendance; new, more stringent attendance policies and truancy procedures were developed to coincide with educational objectives and changes in the law.

The results were not unexpected. The volume of truancy referrals to court increased dramatically: In the 1983–84 academic year, there were 1,332 referrals, 825 from Minneapolis schools. For Minneapolis, this was a 100 percent increase over the previous academic year high (1977–78); it was 500 more than in the year prior to the change in the law.

The implications were soon apparent: The volume inhibited the court's ability to individualize in addressing the problems underlying truant behavior. In response, the court had to use an intervention method that was both easily administered and cost-effective. Processing referrals and maintaining and monitoring accurate attendance records also interfered with the schools' provision of direct services. Both institutions were devoting extensive resources to the process at a time of budgetary restraints. For the first time, the impact of the activities on school attendance was evaluated.

The 1983–84 Truancy Study

The "1983–84 Truancy Study: A Comparison of Court Intervention Strategies and Their Impact on School Attendance" was a project of the Planning and Evaluation Unit, Hennepin County Court Services.[8] Schools collaborated by providing attendance data for the sample.

The research study was designed to compare the effects of two court intervention strategies on the school attendance of adjudicated truants. Specifically, it examined the effectiveness of the favored approach: a lecture, the disposition of four hours on a work squad (unpaid work, in groups), and placement under court observation for 30 days with a warning that further truancy would result in additional hours on a work squad and that chronic truancy could result in out-of-home placement.

For purposes of this discussion, only a brief summary of those findings directly pertinent to truancy intervention planning by the school and court will be presented. It should be noted that, although drawn from all of Hennepin County, 85 percent of the sample consisted of MPS students.

Of a total sample of 150, 115 were first-time truants. Sixty-six received no time on a work squad, only observation. Forty-nine were place on a work squad (four hours of unpaid work).

Thirty-five youths had prior truancies. Results are based on 137 out of 150 cases—a 91 percent response rate.

- 79 percent of the first-time truants receiving the disposition of no work squad were absent without excuse at least seven times during the 60-day follow-up period. The average number of days truant for these recidivists was 19, or almost four weeks of school.

- 77 percent of the first-time truants receiving the disposition of work squad were truant at least seven times during the follow-up period. The average number of days truant for this group was 22. No significant differences were found between the two disposition groups under study.

- Almost 8 percent of the youths with previous truancies were truant seven or more days during the follow-up period, with the average number of days truant being 21.

- Approximately one-third of the youths under study were truant from school the *very next day* after appearing in court.

- Of the first-time truants with seven or more unexcused absences, only 52 percent were referred to court for a second citation during the follow-up period. This indicates that nearly half of the juveniles who continued to be truant after their adjudication hearings were not being returned to court despite their continued disregard for the compulsory attendance law.

- First-time truants who did not have any unexcused absences during the first week after court were less likely to be recidivist than those who displayed truant behavior during this time period.[9]

MPS 1983–84 Truancy Procedures and Statistics

MPS has developed formal documented procedures that are carried out concurrently with informal school-based intervention strategies. Throughout the process, school social workers and other staff may telephone parents, make home visits, provide counseling, refer students for special education assessment, and seek assistance from other school and community resources.

Formal procedures include the following: (1) A principal's letter is sent to parent(s) after three days of unexcused absence. (2) After seven days, a letter from an MPS attorney is sent to parent(s) warning that the youth has broken the compulsory attendance law, that the youth and parent(s) may be held legally responsible for this behavior, and that private data will be released if a citation is written. (3) If truancy continues, after five more calendar days, a citation for truancy is written by the school's police liaison officer.

In 1983–84, there were 825 referrals made to the court; 1,529 letters were sent to parents by the attorney for the district. Consistently, this letter—albeit controversial because it delayed immediate referral—appeared to be an effective deterrent. Some 46 percent of truants who received the letter in 1983–84 were not referred on to court.

Of the MPS students referred to court, 50 percent came from junior high schools, 35 percent from senior high schools, and 15 percent from elementary schools. Because of the recognition that parental responsibility is highest at the elementary level, the court refers elementary-aged students to Hennepin County Community Services, Protective Services. Referred students were truant an average of 12.8 full days and 7.7 partial days at the point of referral. The district has significantly reduced the number of days students are truant before referral in recent years. The referred students' average age was 13.4. In elementary schools, two-thirds of referred students were boys, but by junior and senior high school, boys and girls were equally truant. In 1983–84, some 36 percent of MPS students were minority Americans. Minority representation among referred students in elementary and junior high schools was significantly disproportionate (63 and 49 percent, respectively). The percentage of minority Americans referred in senior high schools was less disproportionate (33 percent). Although 6 percent of MPS students were Asian American, and generally recent immigrants to the country, only five were referred for truancy. Referral forms completed by school personnel indicated that 79 percent of referred students were from single-parent families; 37 percent of the general school population were from single-parent families.

Using the county's sample drawn from Minneapolis schools (127 students), a survey of centralized special education records showed that 34 percent of students had received some level of special education services while enrolled in the district. Because resources did not allow a thorough review of individual records to discern nondistrict services, it is likely that this represents a minimal estimate.

When preparing referrals, social workers were instructed to document school programs and services used to remediate truancy. School social work was listed as "program used" in 66 percent of all referrals, and generally an average of two programs listed for each referral. Referral to a variety of community agencies was the most frequent service provided (546 referrals). The data collected indicated that, in almost all cases, the social worker or another school staff member had contacted parents, and that schools were seeking assistance from school programs and community resources before making referrals to the court.

Implications for Planning

All data showed that the school district had increased its use of the court, although information collected generally substantiated claims that it was used as a last resort in those cases in which other school and community interventions had failed. Certainly both institutions were allocating significant resources to the process. School and court practitioners and officials were concerned, however, that the volume of cases, and lack of adequate resources, precluded individualization and direct services at all levels of intervention. Moreover, a classic double-bind existed: If schools used the court as a last resort, the number of days a student was truant before referral increased; the court then truly saw the "habitual truant" for whom it had a diminished effect because of limited resources. Conversely, if MPS referred truant students immediately, the court would have seen them early, but would have been overwhelmed by their number. The school, better able to solve the problem, would have relinquished the opportunity to intervene.

Data collected by both school and court corroborated the supposition that truancy should be viewed as a "signal for attention." The number of students who received special education services or referrals to family, mental health, or chemical treatment agencies and the characteristics of students truant in Minneapolis schools point to a high-risk population.

The court, in summary, saw students with habitual truant behavior, generally symptomatic of other complex problems. Its responses were constrained by statute and resources. Obviously, with nearly 80 percent recidivism, the juvenile court was not having the effect intended. The school district—although decreasing truant behavior in some of its students—had been unable to divert 825 young people from the juvenile justice system. This high-risk group needed more individualized attention and intervention than either system had to offer.

Finally, the dimension of the problem went beyond the purview of the school and the court: The problem also belonged to the family. For this group of students, however, it is likely that families too were stressed. The repercussions of unattended truancy for society may be reflected in future welfare, unemployment, and correctional statistics. Thus, truancy was—and remains—a community problem.

The 1984–85 Truancy Pilot Project

Minneapolis officials were unwilling to abandon their joint commitment to collaboration in truancy interventions. School and court officials used the data they had collected to develop a model that used resources more effectively and efficiently.

Target Population
The school district concentrated its resources in junior high schools. Since the average truant was 13 years old, more referrals came from junior high schools. There was more potential for involving parents and intervening before truant behavior became habitual. Young adolescents were more amenable to caring adult relationships, role models, and behavior change.

Primary Strategies

Two pilot junior high schools were selected for implementation of all strategies. However, all six junior high schools and two elementary schools were assigned truancy intervention workers and truancy clerks, in addition to already assigned school social workers.

Two Hennepin County Court Services professional case aides were assigned to the pilot schools. With functions similar to probation officers, they provide case management and direct services to pilot school students referred to court for truancy.

Pilot Objectives

The pilot project has primary objectives: (1) to view truancy as a signal for attention and a reflection of unresolved problems within the student, the home, the school, and the community; (2) to individualize pretruancy and posttruancy interventions to meet the unique needs of students; (3) to involve parents and community agencies in encouraging school attendance; (4) to team at the building level in implementing truancy interventions; (5) to provide consistent and prompt posthearing follow-up to assure return to school; (6) to divert students from entering the juvenile justice system; and (7) to reduce the incidence of out-of-home placements.

Interventions

There are four intervention levels.

Level I.   *Comprehensive building of the truancy team's prevention and support interventions aimed at improving the attendance of all students.* The truancy team includes the school social worker, truancy intervention worker, assistant principal, court case aide, and school counselor. Interventions may include an accurate attendance maintenance system, sharing of attendance expectations with the student body and parents, court presentations to the student body, contingency programs for good attendance, and mobilization of support from community agencies and local businesses.

Level II.   *Early identification and intervention for those students identified by team members as high truancy risks.* Interventions may include attendance monitoring, student counseling, personal contacts with parent(s), scheduling/classroom modifications, referral to school and community resources, and MPS principal's letter to parent(s) after three days of unexcused absence.

Level III.   Truancy intervention process initiated for students identified as truant. If there is no improvement in attendance following parent(s) receipt of the attorney's warning letter, for first-time truants, a school-based panel meeting is requested by the school and court. Panel participants include the school truancy team, parent(s), and student. The purposes of the school-based panel meeting are to review attendance, share consequences of continued truancy, assess needs, explore resources and options, make recommendations, develop a contract, and assign a case manager. The student's adherence to the contract will be monitored following the panel meeting.

Level IV.   Court surveillance for students who continue to be truant and are referred to juvenile court. Case aides attend a hearing and, following disposition, monitor and follow up to assure the student returns to school the *next day,* and/or rerefer the student if truancy continues. During the observation period, the case aide works closely with truancy team members, parent(s), the student, and agency personnel to encourage school attendance.

Implications for Practice

Truant behavior is a "red flag" for needed intervention. The image of the early truant officer may diminish social workers' interest in this area. Nonetheless, it is likely that, under most circumstances, this group of students would be referred to the school social worker. The MPS students identified as truant in 1983–84 were certainly at risk. A significant number had been referred for special education services at some time in their school career, and this substantiates the contention that even when social work funding is based on services to handicapped students, truancy intervention is an appropriate function.

Skepticism of this approach to truancy intervention is appropriate. Certainly school and court practitioners and officials in Minneapolis continually question the efficacy of court intervention given its effect on actual attendance. The focus on attendance can be viewed, however, as a screening function allowing social workers to identify students who need assistance. Because of the process, many students—including those not included in the referred group of 825—are referred for school and community services or provided with other school support. Many more parents became aware of their children's school problems, and were involved at some level in addressing them. Without the process, many needs might go undetected.

School districts employ social workers to support their educational mission. Because of current exigencies, school social workers are being called on to demonstrate their contribution to achievement of educational goals. Nowhere are social work services more clearly tied to these goals than in attendance and truancy work.

Social workers assigned to elementary and junior high schools should be constantly alert to truancy patterns that are developing. All MPS experience points to the necessity of early intervention. When the patterns have become well established, the combined resources of school and court rarely penetrate them.

Experience has also shown that a team approach to truancy intervention is advantageous. Truancy intervention workers—essentially paraprofessional positions—have significantly increased the school's ability to reach out to parents and monitor daily attendance. Much of truancy work is clerical and routine follow-up; its functions are appropriate for differentiated staffing. Concomitantly, the professional component is vital: Because of the complex problems of which truancy is symptomatic the professional social worker's assessment, treatment, and referral skills are essential. It is at this point that students may be identified as needing special education services or referral to treatment or social agencies. When blended, the functions and skills of both combine for effective intervention.

If, as suggested, truancy is a community problem, school social workers are in an optimal position to intervene. With their base in the school, they have traditionally been the link to the home and community agencies. School social workers are trained and experienced in outreach. It is the key ingredient in any successful truancy program.

Finally, school social workers must be advocates in a school district's truancy program—certainly advocates for individual students at all intervention levels. Just as important, however, is advocacy for a continuum of interventions ranging from those provided by school and community to those mandated by the court. Some educators, and social workers as well, believe that truancy is the court's problem. It is the law-and-order approach: "Get them to court." Bypassing school interventions not only abdicates school responsibility, but plays the "trump card" first. In Minnesota, because dispositional alternatives for adjudicated truants are limited by statute and juvenile courts are overburdened, the court is not in the best position to intervene. Early aggressive interventions by the school, using home and community assistance, should be the first choice. When that fails, court intervention may be warranted and needed as a last resort.

Notes and References

1. J. T. Johnson, "A Truancy Program: The Child Welfare Agency and the School," *Child Welfare*, 55 (September–October 1976), pp. 573–580.

2. R. S. Levine, "An Assessment Tool for Early Intervention in Cases of Truancy," *Social Work in Education*, 6 (Spring 1984), pp. 133–150.

3. R. C. Compton, "Diagnostic Evaluation of Committed Delinquents," in B. L. Kratoville, ed., *Youth in Trouble: A Symposium* , May 2-3, 1974, Dallas, Tex. (San Rafael, Calif.: Academic Therapy Publications, 1975), pp. 50–51.

4. A. J. Mauser, "Learning Disabilities and Delinquent Youth," *Academic Therapy* (Summer 1974); reprinted in Kratoville, ed., *Youth in Trouble*, pp. 91–102.

5. W. H. Miller and E. Windhauser, "Reading Disability: Tendency Toward Delinquency?" *The Clearing House*, 46 (November 1971), pp. 183–186.

6. Office of Assistant Secretary for Planning and Evaluation, *What You Should Know about Educational Handicaps and Delinquency*, Juvenile Justice Tapes, (Washington, D.C.: U.S. Department of Health, Education & Welfare, 1974).

7. M. J. Smetanka, "Minneapolis Schools Planning to Toughen Truancy Program," *Minneapolis Star and Tribune*, September 12, 1984.

8. P. M. Lantz, "1983–84 Truancy Study: A Comparison of Court Intervention Strategies and Their Impact on School Attendance" (Minneapolis, Minn.: Planning and Evaluation Unit, Hennepin County Court Services, September 1984). (Photocopied.)

9. Ibid.

A Summer Employment Project for an Alternative School

Don Bebee
Betty Guhman
Carol Ethridge

As the spring school semester drew to a close and summer approached, students at the local alternative high school began the usual anxious discussion about employment. Comments included "I don't know where to begin." "It's useless—I'll never get a good job." "I've just got to find something." The overall mood was pessimistic at best, students held little hope of finding a job of any kind.

THIS SCENE IS NOT ATYPICAL among junior and senior high school students and is particularly common in the alternative school population. Summer jobs for high school students are hard to find in a college town, but the employment-related problems of the alternative school population extend beyond job availability. A variety of work-related limitations or "handicaps" encountered by this population must also be considered. In order to address the employment needs of these youths, it became apparent that it would be necessary not only to assist them in finding jobs but, perhaps more important, to address those handicaps that would otherwise continue to affect their work potential in the future.

The resulting project as described in this article represents a unique approach to addressing the employment-related problems and needs of the alternative school population. It also represents a linkage of efforts, resources, and expertise in a university community; this involved an alternative public high school (Uptown

School), a private nonprofit therapeutic day care facility (Children's House), and the Social Work Program at the University of Arkansas in Fayetteville. The project was designed to provide summer employment and job skills training and development for students from Uptown School, who were subsequently trained and hired as teacher's aides at the Children's House facility.

Uptown School, with a capacity to serve thirty students between the ages of 14 and 18, is funded and administered by the Fayetteville Public School system. Uptown was designed to address the unique needs of students who are considered by the regular schools to be at "high risk" as potential school dropouts. It has been both a leader and a model for communities in Arkansas interested in developing alternative school programs.

Children's House is a therapeutic day care facility operated under the auspices of the Economic Opportunity Agency of Washington County. The program at Children's House is designed to provide therapeutic intervention and day care services to children between the ages of 18 months and 6 years. All of the children are active protective services cases from either Arkansas Social Services or S.C.A.N. (Suspected Child Abuse and Neglect).

The Social Work Program is an undergraduate program at the University of Arkansas–Fayetteville Campus, Fulbright College of Arts and Sciences. In this program, considerable emphasis is placed upon experiential endeavors as a companion to theoretical teachings in a classroom setting. Faculty have been actively involved with both Uptown School and Children's House, providing ongoing program support and consultation and routinely utilizing both programs for senior internship placements and volunteer work assignments.

Problem Statement

The alternative school student population at Uptown School is, by definition, at high risk in a variety of personal and interpersonal areas and therefore in need of special attention and support. Of particular concern to this project is the recognition that, in the area of work, these students have extensive limitations or handicaps when compared to students in the regular school population. These handicaps include, but are not limited to, the following: lack of orientation to the world of work, high unemployment risk, lack of job-readiness skills, lack of a work history, and high dropout potential. In addition, these students must supplement their family and personal incomes through outside employment, adding further stress and complication to the expressed handicap. These students can also be described as coming from chaotic family and home environments, having been exposed to poor parenting models, having a lack of knowledge and skills in the area of child care and development, and being at risk for early marriage and/or pregnancy. The population being described appears to have a significant "failure" orientation and lack of self-confidence. There also is an identifiable limit on the part of the students in regard to knowledge of and access to community resources that might aid in meeting many of the above-mentioned needs.

Project Goals

Although the project was directed primarily toward the employment problems and needs of Uptown School students, program planning and development opportunities for social work students and the summer staffing needs of Children's House were also addressed. Children's House has a great need for volunteers within its program, because its low budget results in limited staffing. Because the program depends heavily on students from the University of Arkansas, this need becomes even more critical in the summer due to the general drop in volunteerism during that time.

Project goals and objectives included the following:

1. To increase the financial resources of Uptown School students through the funding of a program to hire ten students as summer teacher's aides at Children's House.

2. To increase the job readiness skills of potential participants through a pre-employment job training and orientation to the world of work series.

3. To increase future employability of selected student participants through on-the-job training, supervision, and support as Children's House teacher's aides.

4. To increase student participants' parenting skills and knowledge base through classroom instruction in child development and supervised work experience with children.

5. To increase student participants' self-concept in regard to work through individual support and guidance and the opportunity for positive growth training.

6. To increase student participants' awareness and knowledge of community resources through field trips, discussions, and presentations by local community agency or organization representatives.

7. To increase the summer staff/child ratio at Children's House through the development and funding of ten teacher's aide positions.

8. To provide an opportunity for social work students to become involved in the design, funding, implementation, and evaluation of a model youth summer employment project.

Basic Program Design

The overall design for the project required the joint efforts and cooperation of Uptown School, Children's House, and the Social Work Program. The components of pre-employment training, job interviewing, job orientation, inservice training, ongoing evaluation and feedback, plus work scheduling and time for daily supervision/training had to be addressed to heighten the chances of the students' success. Awareness that funding might present a problem led to development of realistic minimum budget requirements and a variety of possible funding sources.

The budget included salaries for a full-time supervisor for the project (forty hours per week at $5.00 per hour) and for ten teacher's aides (thirty hours per week at $3.35 per hour). The project ran for ten weeks with the project supervisor being employed for twelve weeks. Additional miscellaneous expenses were built-in with the end result being a relatively low-cost summer project that totaled $14,510.72, or $1,491.07 per participant. Numerous funding possibilities were considered; the new JTPA (Job Training Partnership Act) that replaced CETA (Comprehensive Employment and Training Act) appeared the most feasible and easiest to gain access to. Negotiations with JTPA resulted in total project funding.

Preemployment Training

Social work students, under the guidance and supervision of faculty, developed and conducted a sixteen-hour mini-course aimed at job readiness. This course was open to all Uptown students, and graduates of the course became the pool from which applicants for the teacher's aide positions were chosen. The course itself included two basic components. The first component provided a general orientation to the world of work; it included such topics as interviewing for jobs, work expectations, employer/employee relations, and appropriate and inappropriate behaviors. The second component focused on basic parenting skills and interactions with preschool-age children. These sessions addressed such topics as general child development, basic discipline, positive interaction, and communication skills in addition to specific characteristics and needs of the Children's House residents.

Selection of Participants

The Uptown students who successfully completed the sixteen-hour pre-employment training course were then eligible to apply for the ten teacher's aide positions. Each applicant was interviewed by a three-person team consisting of representatives from Children's House, Uptown School, and the University of Arkansas Social Work Program. The interview process was designed to screen applicants as well as provide interview experience for the students.

Orientation

Prior to actual placement as a teacher's aide within Children's House, the ten students chosen were required to complete ten hours of orientation training. This training was conducted by the Children's House staff and included particulars of the job assignments along with detailed job expectations. This time was used to acquaint students with both staff and children, and to begin the process of familiarizing students with the information needed to work effectively with the children. Time was also allowed for overall program observation along with assigned classroom time according to the age group with which the student would be working.

On-the-Job Training

Although the students had undergone a concentrated sixteen-hour pre-employment training and a ten-hour orientation, they continued to receive training while on the job. Each work week consisted of ten hours of training in daily two-hour sessions. Training topics can be generally categorized as: (1) job-readiness skills; (2) appropriate on-the-job behavior; (3) parenting skills and knowledge; (4) community resources and support systems; and (5) personal growth and development.

Specific training topics related to these categories included

1. Job Readiness

   - Identifying career interests and aptitudes
   - Identifying possible job opportunities

- Resume writing
- Successful interviewing
- Securing reference letters

2. Appropriate On-the-Job Behavior
   - Dealing with supervisors
   - Accepting criticism
   - Effective communication techniques
   - Employer expectations: attendance and punctuality
   - Appropriate dress and grooming

3. Parenting Skills and Knowledge
   - Age-appropriate expectations
   - Discipline without hitting
   - Power of positive reinforcement
   - Family planning
   - Effect of room arrangement on children's behavior

4. Community Resources and Support Systems
   - Financial assistance for education and job training
   - Public use of university facilities
   - Counseling and psychological services
   - Local and regional education/job-training programs and institutions
   - Fayetteville Public Library programs and services

5. Personal Growth and Development
   - Assertiveness training
   - Interpersonal communication skills
   - Developing a positive self-image
   - Planning for the future
   - Personal problem-solving techniques

Supervision and Support
 In addition to the daily group-training sessions, particular emphasis was placed upon individual supervision and support for each student. A primary responsibility of the project director was

to monitor the progress and problems of each student and to provide individual attention and support as needed. Written evaluations of each participant's job performance were submitted to the project supervisor weekly by the Children's House staff.

Areas of evaluation included attendance, work habits, attitudes and appearance, dependability, and relationships with people. Careful review and analysis of these evaluations with the students provided an excellent opportunity to identify weaknesses and problem areas, as well as a chance to offer positive reinforcement for job-appropriate behavior.

Program Outcomes

The outcomes related to the primary program goals as assessed by the project supervisor, Children's House staff, and student participants included the following:

Outcome 1. Increase in Financial Resources of Students
The majority of the participants (five out of ten) were essentially self-supporting, and the little income they had generally had been consumed by basic living expenses. In the past, they had been dependent on incomes from a variety of odd jobs, the erratic and unpredictable nature of which made it very difficult to budget effectively or establish savings. This first experience with stabilized incomes resulted in an increased ability to schedule activities in advance, a reduction of anxiety concerning prompt payment of debts, and the expansion of recreational outlets. Average earnings per student amounted to $938 for the ten-week period.

Related training sessions included: a trip to the Court House to obtain legal identification for minors, information on establishing checking and saving accounts, and discussions on effective low income budgeting.

Outcome 2. Increase in Job-Readiness Skills
Students had attended twenty-six hours of pre-employment training prior to job placement at Children's House. These sessions included instruction in job-readiness skills as well as basic child development information. Pretests and posttests were administered in each of these areas to gauge the effectiveness of this training.

The results from the pretest indicated students had a fairly good grasp of subject matter for both job skills and child care. The mean score was 82.36 with a median of 84. The posttest showed a solid improvement with a mean score of 94.18 and a median score of 96. Definite overall improvement was seen, although the group may have known the "do's and don'ts" well from the start and simply may have had trouble with the application.

Presentations had been made by the director and the volunteer coordinator of Children's House on information relating to the nature and goals of therapeutic day care and, more specifically, the role of teacher's aides. Both staff and participants viewed this preliminary introduction to the expectations of the employer as instrumental in reducing the level of insecurity, stress, and confusion normally experienced by new employees in the first week of employment.

Participants appeared to feel an increased level of commitment to and investment in their positions as teacher's aides due to the time spent in training and preparation for those positions.

Outcome 3. Increase in Future Employability

Job skills training had been an ongoing and major component of the project. This training involved not only feedback and consultation on positive and negative aspects of current work performance but also an emphasis on how the skills being developed might influence and be applicable to future employability and job performance. Related training sessions included such topics as job search, interviewing successfully, resume writing, requesting letters of reference, job-appropriate behavior and dress, acceptance of criticism, and career planning.

Written evaluations of the participants, submitted weekly by the Children's House staff, documented the growth and skill development of the participants as they assumed greater confidence and willingness to accept (and demand!) increased responsibility in the classrooms. The evaluations also served to pinpoint problems areas, which could be dealt with in a timely and nonthreatening manner during training.

Perhaps the greatest measure of increased employability lies in the fact that, following termination of the project, three of the participants were hired in various part-time capacities to work for Children's House during the school year.

Outcome 4. Increase in Parenting Skills and Knowledge

Dramatic changes developed in the attitudes of participants in relationship to the children over the course of the project. Although the students displayed much affection and caring from the beginning, they also expressed a great deal of fear about being left alone with the children. By the second half of the ten-week period, participants were confident in their ability to handle emergency situations and to anticipate and understand the needs (spoken and unspoken) of the children.

Related training sessions included such topics as discipline without hitting, age-appropriate expectations in child development; the power of positive reinforcement; childless or childfree—the decision to parent; presentation by Planned Parenthood; incest and sexual abuse of children; children of alcoholics; and the effect of room arrangement on children's behavior.

Upon entering the project, participants tended to view parenthood as an inevitability rather than a choice. As a result of group discussions and related presentations, the majority of participants came to view parenting as a decision and a commitment. Moreover, the decision not to parent was viewed as an acceptable one.

Outcome 5. Improved Self-Concept with Regard to Work or Career

Although an improved self-concept is often difficult to assess, positive attitudinal and behavioral changes in participants were observed by the supervisor and staff. These included

- Willingness to accept work-related criticism with decreased defensiveness

- Increased self-motivation and less reliance on the supervisor to assign tasks

- Increased willingness to undertake projects and assignments foreign to previous experience

- Increased acknowledgment of and willingness to make use of personal skills in classroom projects (carpentry, printing, storytelling, and so forth)

- Less defensiveness in dealing with authority figures and adults in general

These developments were well documented in written weekly evaluations of the participants by the teachers and indicated a striking increase in overall self-confidence. For many of the participants, this was a first experience with successful completion of a task or project. Staff members were extremely conscientious in terms of rewarding responsible behavior with praise and increased levels of responsibility and privilege. This approach, primarily positive reinforcement of job-appropriate behavior, seems to have contributed in large part to the success of the project.

Outcome 6. Increase in Awareness and Knowledge of Community Resources
    Because of the special needs and problems of Uptown students, as identified earlier, a working knowledge of community resources was deemed to be of particular importance. To address that need, a number of field trips and presentations by direct-service agencies and organizations were scheduled. Trips included: Public Health Department, Chamber of Commerce, Fayetteville Youth Center, University of Arkansas Financial Aid Office, University of Arkansas Athletic Complex, Fayetteville Public Library, Career Planning and Placement Office, and Mullins Library. Presentations were given by local service agencies, including Alateen, Planned Parenthood, Rape Crisis, the Women's Shelter, Ozark Guidance Center, and the Crisis Line.

Outcome 7. Increase in the Staff/Child Ratio at Children's House in the Summer Months
    Enrollment at Children's House was at maximum capacity for the duration of the project. Prior to the students' involvement, the projected staff/child ratio was approximately 2:7 per classroom. Student participant involvement increased that ratio to approximately 4.5:7. This increase freed teachers to make home visits and to complete paperwork as needed. The increase in ratio also allowed for greater individualized attention. Participants were able to carry out activities and projects created by the teachers to meet the specific needs of individual children.

Outcome 8. Opportunity for Social Work Students to Become Involved in the Design, Implementation, and Evaluation of a Model Summer Employment Project for Youths
    The Social Work Program at the University of Arkansas emphasizes integrating theoretical classroom teaching with experiential opportunities planned to enhance overall learning. Since much of the focus is on preparing students for employment at the B.A. level, a considerable amount of energy is put into arranging practical work endeavors to complement their learning.
    This project allowed several social work students the opportunity to contribute to the successful implementation of the Uptown/

Children's House summer program. One of the authors, a senior social work student, took primary responsibility for the design and coordination of the project. This included communicating about the overall program design with the social work interns at both Uptown and Children's House and providing, with assistance from another senior social work major, the sixteen-hour period of training at Uptown. In addition, the project supervisor was a returning social work major who was cited as being key to the success of the project.

Social work students were involved in the design, training, supervision, implementation, and evaluation of the project. All gave feedback that evidenced both personal and professional gains as a result of their involvement.

Discussion and Conclusions

A review of project goals and related outcome measures indicates a highly successful model. Personal feedback reveals that numerous benefits were reaped by the student participants, the Children's House program staff and children, and the involved social work students. Clearly assessing the lasting effect on the student participants is difficult at this point. It is anticipated, however, that the documented increase in positive work experience and positive self-esteem will lead to future employment successes. In addition, the increased skills and knowledge related to child rearing are expected to influence positively the students' parenting abilities.

The original decision to use Children's House as the training location was based upon the assumption that the Uptown students would bring with them a unique understanding and appreciation for the home-related problems encountered by the children. The fact that many of them had grown up in largely chaotic homes was expected to provide them with a very special preparation for this type of work. Feedback from Children's House teachers and staff indicated that this did indeed occur. In their roles of teacher's aides, the students consistently displayed a special level of patience and responsiveness to the children.

Several key components can be identified as critical to the success of this project and should be carefully considered by other communities interested in duplication. These include: (1) requirement of pre-employment and orientation training; (2) provision of individual support and guidance by a full-time program supervisor; and (3) daily group-training sessions.

Although the pre-employment and orientation training sessions initially appeared lengthy and time consuming, they set the stage for a serious employment and training opportunity. The clear delineation of job expectations and requirements prior to assuming on-the-job responsibilities and duties reduced anxiety levels of the students and provided a much-needed introduction to the world of work. Most important, this allowed the students to get off to a good start.

A second critical factor was the inclusion of a full-time project supervisor. Although the responsibility for direct on-the-job supervision of the aides was provided by Children's House staff, additional (and *critical*) individual support and guidance was provided by the project supervisor. Her careful attention to the progress and problems of each participant was clearly seen as a success factor.

The third factor involved the requirement of daily in-service training. These sessions provided for the successful integration of newly acquired knowledge and on-the-job experience, resulting in both work-related skill development and positive personal growth.

In considering the possibility of duplication in other communities, this model appears to offer several positive features. The model addresses several key problems and needs experienced by the alternative school population (e.g., employability, parenting skills, self-confidence) within a single program. The client populations and program resources (alternative school and day care) exist and are easily accessible in most communities. Funding for such programs could be accessed through a variety of sources, including the local school system, local JTPA council, the state's Juvenile Justice and Delinquency Prevention Advisory Group, and a variety of other state and local public and private funding sources. The cooperative nature of the project should prove to be a "selling" point to potential funding sources.

Project ALIVE: A Primary Prevention Model for Adolescent Suicide

Debra M. Meckley

UNFORTUNATELY, THE ISSUE OF adolescent suicide is not seriously addressed in many schools until after such a tragedy occurs or a serious attempt is made. It is at that point that school administrators turn to school social workers and mental health professionals to ask for advice in the "postvention" aspect of the suicide. It is also at that point that those school social workers and mental health professionals can turn short-term tertiary prevention into long-term primary prevention.

The abovementioned chain of events was the precipitant to the development of Project ALIVE (Actually Life Is Very Exciting): Teenage Suicide Prevention, a joint effort between schools and a family service agency aimed at the primary prevention of adolescent suicide. This article will describe the initial development of the project, the strategies and rationale involved in implementing the project, and the components of the project.

Initial Development of the Project

Project ALIVE evolved over the course of three years. The first involvement of the family service agency and a school system in regard to adolescent suicide occurred after the suicide of a student in that school system. School administrators and faculty members were receptive to postvention by social workers due to their uncertainty about handling student reactions to the suicide. Interventions at that point involved an inservice program with teachers and administrators and classroom discussions for students, all of which were conducted by a social worker. Prior to the classroom discussions, students were asked to write down questions that they had about adolescent suicide.

Approximately nine months later, this same format was used by the family service agency in another school district where there had been a series of suicide attempts within a short period of time. Again, students were asked to write down their questions about suicide. In both situations, social workers used the questions in classroom discussions to address thoroughly students' concerns.

The Study-Action Team

A total of approximately seven hundred students had submitted ninety-two different questions related to suicide. After examining and collating the questions, the decision was made to turn them over to the family service agency's advocacy program. The purpose would be to set up a committee, or Study-Action Team, to analyze the need for increased education and services on adolescent suicide prevention and to determine methods for fulfilling that need. The Study-Action Team consisted of an agency social worker, mental health professionals, teachers, and parents.

After studying the county served by the family service agency, the Study-Action Team concluded that many school districts were not adequately addressing the problem of adolescent suicide in their curriculum but were dealing with individual students experiencing emotional difficulties. The group also concluded that although community resources and expertise were available to schools, they were generally used for intervention and postvention by schools rather than for prevention.

A study of the literature on suicide and primary prevention in mental health was also conducted. The conclusion of this study indicated several important factors later included in the Project ALIVE model. These factors were integral to the success of any proposed action aimed at addressing the study conclusions.

One concern of the Study-Action Team was with schools' receptivity to a primary prevention program. For Project ALIVE to be successful, schools had to be receptive to broadening the scope of their involvement in adolescent suicide prevention. In a study of nine school systems, Jason found that school personnel are most receptive to primary prevention programs when they perceive that there is a need for the program, when the various aspects of the program are thoroughly explained, and when the suggested program is seen as a "positive, educational, competency-enhancing experience."[1]

Another concern of the Study-Action Team was to substantiate the primary prevention approach to adolescent suicide. In examining literature from the 1960s, 1970s, and 1980s, the team found that one common theme emerged, that is, the need to be aware of the prodromal symptoms of suicide.[2] Schneidman proposed that efforts be made by communities using all forms of media to educate about the warning signs of suicide and about community resources available for those needing help.[3]

Historically, suicide prevention centers, or hotlines, were believed to be an effective means of suicide prevention; however, these centers were most often used by individuals of low suicidal risk.[4] Perhaps seriously suicidal individuals were unaware of the available service and therefore did not use it, or perhaps they did not feel the service would be of help to them. Whatever the reason, the most important factor in primary prevention seems to be community effort. Caplan defined the focus of primary prevention as the community.[5] The community must be involved in providing effective suicide intervention services, in making the public aware of those services, and in educating people about the appropriate use of those services. Primary prevention does not involve waiting for the suicidal individual to contact a prevention center but outreach to the individual through education of the community about suicide warning signs.

Components of the Project

Given the abovementioned results of the study, the Study-Action Team decided to develop a lesson plan that could be used for educating adults and students about adolescent suicide. The lesson plan, Project ALIVE: Teenage Suicide Prevention, was based on the questions posed by students in middle schools and high schools. The questions most frequently asked were:

1. Why do people commit suicide?

2. How do you deal with a person who has attempted suicide when he or she comes back to school?

3. What should you do if a friend tells you he or she is thinking about committing suicide?

4. What ways are there to deal with stress, anger, depression, and tension?

5. What are the warning signs of suicide?

6. What do people use to try to commit suicide?

7. How do you deal with parents who "get on your back" all the time when it does not help to try to talk to them?

8. How many suicides are there in the United States over a period of time?

9. Is suicide a mental illness?

10. What happens to the person who has attempted suicide and failed?

11. How do you know if someone is serious or not when he or she talks about suicide?

12. Where do you go if you have a problem?

13. How do you handle your problems without hurting yourself?

14. Does the person who is attempting suicide really want to die?

15. Do you think that people who attempt suicide will try again?

To address these questions, sections were included in the lesson plan on factors contributing to suicide, general statistics of adolescent suicide, warning signs of potentially suicidal adolescents, strategies for helping the troubled teenager, coping skills for teenagers, and telephone numbers and descriptions of available community resources. These portions of the lesson plan would be useful for any age group in understanding, identifying, and helping the suicidal adolescent.

Because the target population for prevention were teenagers, schools were the logical focal point of initial intervention.[6] Additional sections were included in the lesson plan offering suggestions and classroom activities for teachers and outlines of the above sections that could be reproduced as student handouts. In addition to this teacher's packet, an audiocassette tape of a play depicting a girl's suicide attempt and a discussion of basic information about adolescent suicide was produced as a teaching aid. (It should be noted that the play was edited by middle school students in an effort to make it more meaningful to that age group. Students also read, for recording, the appropriate parts of the play.)

This format for the lesson plan was developed to overcome the potential obstacle of teacher resistance. For the teacher who would be very interested and comfortable in teaching about adolescent suicide, a wealth of teaching resources would be available in the lesson plan. For the extremely resistant or uncomfortable teacher, the cassette tape could provide an acceptable level of instruction with minimal teacher involvement.

The major obstacle to overcome in making the lesson plan a primary prevention model was convincing school administrators and faculty who were not in the anguish of a suicide crisis that this information would be requested and needed by their students. Another common obstacle was the concern that talking about suicide would give students the idea to try suicide.

To address these concerns, an in-service program was provided to school district superintendents and semiannual in-service programs are offered to teachers. The in-service programs are conducted by members of the Study-Action Team, with the goal of the programs being twofold: educational and supportive. Although the information part of the in-service training is important, the supportive element seems most effective in addressing and easing resistance to the project. Thus, superintendents and teachers not only gain an understanding of adolescent suicide but also feel an alliance with the family service agency. The schools' participation in Project ALIVE is integral to primary prevention and the identification of potentially suicidal teens, and the family service agency is available to the schools for secondary prevention or treatment. The alliance built serves both parties' purposes.

Summary

It is impossible to know the number of teenagers who may have been helped by Project ALIVE, but it is possible to assess its impact by examining the receptiveness of school systems. In the targeted community, fourteen of sixteen school districts have incorporated the lesson plan into their curriculum, and eight of those fourteen have requested further education for peer counselors and students. In the first two years that the program was in place, 1,803 students and 319 counselors, teachers, administrators, and parents were reached through agency-provided programs. Project ALIVE has also been made available to the church community in an effort to reach more parents of teenagers.

A program such as Project ALIVE can be useful in all stages of prevention. Its effectiveness as a primary prevention model can be attributed to both the product and the process. In order to reach adolescents, the lesson plan had to have connecting elements to that population. Involving adolescents in its development gave it that quality, which made it acceptable to teenagers. Their involvement also helped school administrators realize students' interest in such a program.

The process of building an alliance between schools and community resources also improved the effectiveness of the effort. Schools were not being asked to accept the project in isolation. Instead, the community—other schools, parents, social service agencies, and students—was asking and backing up that request with supportive services. Project ALIVE's strength lies in connected numbers.

Notes and References

1. L. A. Jason, "Prevention in the Schools: Behavioral Approaches," in R. H. Price et al., eds., *Intervention in Mental Health: Research, Policy and Practice* (Beverly Hills, Calif.: Sage Publications, 1980), p. 130.

2. R. H. Seiden, *Suicide Among Youth* (Washington, D.C.: U.S. Government Printing Office, 1969); E. S. Schneidman, "Recent Developments in Suicide Prevention," in Schneidman, N. L. Farberow, and L. E. Litner, *The Psychology of Suicide* (New York: Science House, 1970); and R. W. Maris, *Pathways to Suicide: A Survey of Self-Destructive Behaviors* (Baltimore, Md.: Johns Hopkins University Press, 1981).

3. E. S. Schneidman, "Suicide of Children and Adolescents: A National Problem," in R. McNeer, ed., *Proceedings of Conference on Depression and Suicide in Adolescents and Young Adults* (Fairlee, Vt.: June 1966).

4. M. L. Gorman, "Primary and Secondary Prevention: A Frame of Reference," in D. B. Anderson and L. J. McClean, eds., *Identifying Suicide Potential* (New York: Behavioral Publications, 1971), pp. 57–61.

5. G. Caplan, *Principles of Preventive Psychiatry* (New York: Basic Books, 1964).

6. J. E. Mack and H. Hickler, *Vivienne: The Life and Suicide of an Adolescent Girl* (Boston: Little, Brown & Co., 1981).

Coping with the Ultimate Change: Death of a Family Member

Janice Furman
Judith Pratt

Right in the middle of school, tears come to my eyes. I feel embarrassed and look the other way. My friends don't know what to say to me.

I sit in class and I don't hear anything that's being said. Then I go home and have this huge stack of homework. I can't seem to do anything. Often, it's 11 o'clock at night before I can begin my homework.

It was Brad's birthday. I had no business being in school. All day, all I could see was Brad's face before my eyes.

STATEMENTS LIKE THESE made by students, coupled with reports from guidance counselors, teachers, and concerned parents, alerted us to a need in our school to provide a service for grieving adolescents. What to do about the need and how to do it efficiently and effectively were the basic questions.

The secondary school (grades 7–12) in Fairfax County, Virginia, to which we are assigned as social workers, has an enrollment of about 4,500 students. We share office space and constituency. Frequently, we consult each other about students' needs and appropriate responses. As the high incidence of bereaved students in our population became more apparent, we discussed possible interventions, including formation of a counseling group in the school.

114

Neither consultation with bereavement specialists nor a search of the available literature provided a model for group counseling with bereaved adolescents; therefore, we proceeded to design our own model. We then consulted with other teachers, guidance counselors, and school secretaries to expand the list of grieving students.

This article describes our model for group counseling for bereaved adolescents in a public school setting. Information included is drawn from the current professional expertise and literature. The methodology and procedures were developed by the authors. In addition, the article is designed to enhance awareness of grief issues among adolescents and to provide guidelines for addressing those needs in a group setting.

Acknowledging that each group is unique, dependent upon its members' various stages of recovery, previous group experience, maturity level, death experience, and support systems, there remain certain universalities upon which this paradigm was designed. Developed through trial and error over three years, this model presents a general guideline. (See Table 1, pp. 116–117.)

Pregroup Phase

A personal interview with each potential member of the group, to determine the student's interest in participating and to discuss relevant issues, was held prior to the first group meeting. An information letter was sent to parents requesting permission for their child to participate in the group. Teacher cooperation also was enlisted, because students would miss a different class each week to attend the group on a rotating schedule. Each student was provided with a group schedule for the semester.

During the preformation stage, the grief process and relevant grief issues were the central ingredients in planning the group experience. An outline of pertinent issues and predictable feelings provided direction for facilitating group sessions.

Session One. Following Hartford's notion that group members "must develop trust, reach out to each other, respond to each other before the group can move into the formation stage," the first session begins with a comfort-building exercise.[1] Then, norms are established with particular emphasis on confidentiality to lay the foundation for building trust. Two other norms that are always included are prompt, regular attendance and members' rights to remain silent. As Carol noted during the first session of her senior

Table 1.
Paradigm for a Support Group for Bereaved Adolescents

Phase	Content	Leader's Role	Rationale
Pregroup			
Pregroup	Referral	Solicit referrals	Ensure appropriate membership
	Screening	Interview referred students	Ensure appropriate membership
	Parent and teacher	Prepare, distribute, collect written parent and teacher permission	Enlist support of parents and teachers
	Planning	Peruse pertinent literature; outline salient issues to be covered	Design logical, sound progression of interventions
Session One	Comfort-building exercise	Facilitate	Reduce anxiety level
	Establishing norms	Guide discussion toward universal agreement of norms	Develop trust
	Sharing death experience succinctly	Gently invite members to share who died, when, and how	Establish universality; counter societal taboo
Group Formation			
Session Two	Keepsake sharing	Acknowledge importance of mementos and relationship they symbolize; invite exploration of connected feelings	Develop group cohesiveness and trust by using symbols to safely share inner world affectively
Integration			
Sessions Three and Four	Retelling "the story"	Invite; respond empathically; encourage supportive interaction among members; educate; normalize; monitor effect of adolescent developmental issues; read vignette to stimulate reticent members	Stimulate empathy among members; set in motion curative factor of universality; decathect the loss; educate and normalize about grief reaction
Session Five	Setting goals	Facilitate recognition of issues by asking questions such as "What are some of the things you want to learn about yourself in the grief process?" or "What are your particular concerns about your loss? For example, are you worried about your grades, your relationships?"	Have members assess individual purpose for group participation; connect grief work with general improved functionality

Table 1. (continued)
Paradigm for a Support Group for Bereaved Adolescents

Phase	Content	Leader's Role	Rationale
Group Functioning and Maintenance			
Session Six	Final rites	Facilitate grief management by offering comments such as "Families have different ways of ritualizing a death."	Facilitate grief management by externalizing thoughts and feelings, by receiving empathic support, by learning about bereavement; let the universality of these experiences deepen peer support and networking
Session Seven	Special occasions	Offer comments such as "Special occasions are especially hard during the first year following a loved one's death."	
Session Eight	Unfinished business	Offer comments such as "After someone dies, the survivors often think of things they said or didn't say, did or didn't do, which they wish had been different."	
Session Nine	Changes	Offer comments such as "Lots of things change in families when someone dies."	
Session Ten	Being bereaved	Offer comments such as "People seem to be uncomfortable around those who have experienced a death."	
Session Eleven	Rechanneling energy: balancing the ledger	Facilitate by asking questions such as "What can you do with some of your time and energy that would make you feel a bit better about your loss?"	Teach that loss can be catalyst for growth
Termination			
Session Twelve	Evaluation	Ask questions such as "What have you learned about yourself that has been helpful in other relationships?"	Concretize coping skills; generalize learned material to other life experiences
	Planning post-termination follow-up	Individualize suggestions; invite input from group members	Encourage continued growth and grief management
	Planning celebration	Delegate responsibility for celebration to group: "It's your party!"	
Session Thirteen	Celebration	Celebrate	Ritualize termination
	Highlighting personal growth	Comment on individual members' personal growth; say goodbye	Acknowledge individual strengths; validate the group process

year, after a year's absence from the group, "I hardly said a word in group during my whole sophomore year, but it helped me so much just to be here and listen to others."

Thereafter follows an invitation to students to share their particular death experience, based on the notion that universality or the "disconfirmation of their feelings of uniqueness is a powerful source of relief."[2] As Jenny said upon returning to the group for her second year, "When I first came to this group a month after my mother died, I didn't know anyone who had had a death in the family. To meet people my own age in the same situation was such a relief!" Jenny's comment seems to support Yalom's notion that there is nothing of greater importance for the adolescent than to be included and accepted in some group.[3]

Group Formation Phase

Session Two. The progressive development of group cohesiveness and a safe environment for affective sharing of one's inner world is facilitated during the second session by the sharing of keepsakes or mementos. Recognizing the tenuous group development at this stage and the members' tender feelings, we decided that use of symbols would provide the students with a safe vehicle for an initial limited exposure of grief feelings. Photos, jewelry, poetry, and articles of clothing spur memories and the whole gamut of feelings known to be associated with a grief response: sadness, loneliness, guilt, anger, worry, and fear.

Karen's sadness and sense of loneliness were poignantly evident when she buried her face in her father's sweater and described the comfort these lingering fragrances provided for her. She reported comforting herself in this way when the sadness and loneliness became overwhelming. Recognizing that the sweater may wear out and lose its fragrance, Karen said, "But I'll always have a constant reminder of my father. Everytime I look into the mirror, I see a part of him in me."

Wendy brought a picture of her older sister, who had committed suicide two months earlier. Comments from the group about the two girls' similar appearances led Wendy to divulge, "Everyone always says that we follow one another's footsteps."

The keepsake-sharing technique not only allows students to touch on feelings in a safe environment but also provides leaders with valuable specific concerns of individual group members, thus setting the stage for appropriate interventions. At this stage of group development, bonding and cohesiveness are recognizable by empathic and encouraging group interaction, as well as unsolicited statements about the value of belonging to the group.

Integration Phase

Sessions Three to Five. Continuing the group cohesion-building process by sharing death experiences increases the likelihood of perceived similarities and stimulates empathy and acceptance among members. The curative factor of universality may be set into motion by retelling the story, as nearly as it was experienced, in the supportive group environment. In addition, this has been demonstrated to be an effective means of decathecting the loss.[4] "Retelling the story seems to be a needed source of healing in the process of grief resolution."[5]

Retelling the story and reliving the experience is always painful. Nonetheless, members are usually willing to share in response to a simple invitation by the leaders. The resultant outpouring of emotions provides leaders with an opportunity to model empathic responses and to encourage supportive interaction among group members. Throughout this process, there are ample opportunities for educating the students and normalizing their grief reactions, a process that continues throughout the life span of the group. It is incumbent upon the leaders to monitor continuously the effect of adolescent developmental issues and heightened sensitivity to the loss experience.

Because the retelling is so painful, occasionally there is a member who does not volunteer to tell his or her story. For example, Joanne, whose mother had hanged herself eight years earlier, seemed unable to begin her story. The reading of a vignette that paralleled her experience provided the leaders with an opportunity to engage Joanne gently in talking about her mother's suicide.[6] Lindemann's hypothesis that what is not dealt with is likely to cause problems seems to have been borne out in Joanne's case; she had experienced significant peer, family, and academic problems in the years since her mother's death.[7]

In contrast, Marsha seems to be functioning successfully in all realms of her life. She joined the group three months after her father had died of cancer and reported open sharing with her mother and younger sister about their mutual loss. She was readily able to retell her story in group and experienced an additional source of support as she was learning to manage her grief. As the first anniversary of her father's death approached, Marsha continued to use the group and to express gratitude to her supportive peers, with whom she valued the opportunity to be vulnerable and comforted.

The process of retelling each story is an integrating factor, leaving members ready to assess verbally their purpose and participation in the group.[8] By devoting part of the fifth session to the assessment process, the leaders can direct the students toward connecting their grief work with generalized improved functionality. In addition to the educational aspect of the assessment process, directions for individual and group interventions surface.

Group Functioning and Maintenance Phase

Sessions Six to Ten.   Through the process of sharing keepsakes, retelling the stories, and assessing personal and group goals, many issues of concern arise from the group members. This list predictably includes final rites, special occasions, unfinished business, abrupt and unsought changes, and the difficulties of being a bereaved adolescent. These issues provide the foci for intervention during the group functioning and maintenance phase.[9]

Acknowledging (1) that grief management is facilitated by externalizing thoughts and feelings, by receiving empathic support, and by learning about bereavement, (2) that the adolescent's ego strength is weakened by the struggle to establish his or her identity, resulting in heightened vulnerability to the loss experience, and (3) that loss provides an opportunity for growth, the leaders guide discussion through these five sessions to focus on the salient issues.[10] A myriad of intense and complex emotions emerges in connection with these issues. The leaders' empathic and educational interventions are designed to help members accept these feelings and put them into perspective. Concurrently, the universality of these experiences and feelings deepens peer support and networking. The potential for personal growth is limitless!

A session devoted to final rites can elicit discussion about open or closed caskets, funeral practices, burial, cremation, gatherings after the service, and cemetery visits. In addition to the expected feelings that are generally attached to these events, members share a cross section of other concerns. For example, Karen described her efforts to appear stoic at her father's funeral to counter her grandfather's open weeping. Jan expressed unforgiving and long-lasting rage at family members for their merrymaking following her father's burial. Nicole and Allyson both voiced a desire to visit the cemetery long after the adults in their families perceived a need to take them there. It usually appears that these adolescents feel left out, not consulted, and misunderstood at this juncture, substantiating the notion that young people are often overlooked in the grief process.

Holidays, anniversaries, and other special occasions evoke especially painful feelings during the first year of bereavement. The duration of these intense feelings has been minimized for students who have benefited from early intervention. For others, the intense pain continues to resurface, on occasion after occasion.

Allyson, whose older sister died five years earlier, shared the pain she felt and observed in her family when her sister's birthday coincided with Mother's Day. No one talked about thoughts or feelings in that family. Instead, her mother closeted herself in her room all day, and Allyson kept her sad, confused feelings to herself.

In contrast, Marsha found the first Thanksgiving without her father "okay" and "not nearly as bad as I thought it would be." She anticipated her feelings of emptiness, verbalized them in group, and was able to face the occasion with confidence.

A session in which members face unfinished business with the deceased can be easily launched with a statement such as, "After someone dies, the survivors often think of things they said or didn't say, did or didn't do, which they wish had been different." Students are usually able to personalize this type of statement and share specific experiences. For example, Bruce, whose father was killed in Spain, had decided not to go to the airport with him that last time. Bruce struggled with his never having said goodbye; never having said that last time, "I love you"; and with his guilt about having chosen to be with his friends instead of his family at the airport. When Jan's father, a recovering alcoholic, died suddenly and unexpectedly, the relationship between the two of them was just beginning to prosper. She felt cheated and angry at the termination of this fledgling relationship. The unfinished business issue surfaced frequently for these two bereaved students and appeared to be one factor in their slow, difficult acceptance of loss.

Though the opportunity to reminisce and share important feelings exists when there is an expected death, many students were unable to accept the finality of the illness and consequently seize this opportunity. Jenny, whose mother was dying of cancer, recalled hearing the doctor state the limited time her mother had to live. Jenny's denial prevented her from "tying up loose ends" and saying goodbye. It seems apparent that acknowledging a pending death is counter to an adolescent's feelings of invincibility, thus making unfinished business an issue for all bereaved teenagers.

Sudden and uninvited changes as a result of death affect teenagers in various ways. Family finances concern some, while others find their families more comfortable as a result of insurance payments. In every family, role changes occur. Some adolescents are catapulted into adult roles. They find themselves being auto mechanic, domestic and financial manager, parent to the surviving parent, confidant, and comforter. They are concerned about the widowed parent's emotional status and social life. Some teenagers adamantly object to their parent's consideration of developing new relationships, while others encourage it.

All students address changed attitudes toward life and death as a result of their experience with death. They agree that prior to the death, little time had been spent thinking about the fragility of life, especially their own. However, the experience of losing someone dear triggered a new realization about the unpredictability and delicate balance of life. This maturation was evident in other ways as well. Judith, for example, often initiated discussions among family members in which previously unverbalized feelings and memories of Brad, her 3-year-old drowned brother, were shared.

Awkward and inept interaction between the bereaved and his or her associates is a persistently recurring theme. The question "What does your mother do?" repeatedly caused discomfort for Betty, a ninth grader whose mother had died two years earlier. Karen complained about her best friend's inability to listen to her talk about her father's death. Scott, whose older brother had died suddenly a few months earlier, related an incident in which the boys' coach was unable to engage in any conversation with Scott upon learning of the brother's death. Again and again, group members cited experiences indicating others' discomfort, fear, and avoidance of the bereaved and the topic of death. Within the group, however, members expressed support and listened with apparent comfort to their peers' outpourings of pain.

Sometimes, in the midst of pain, humor can lighten the oppressive mood. It can also be an indicator of progressive healing. For example, Betty speculated about responding to that inevitable question, "What does your mother do?" with "Well, I could say she sleeps a lot!" The resultant laughter in the group provided some levity in the somber setting and evidence that grief can be managed.

Throughout these five sessions, experiences and feelings are relived in a supportive and empathic atmosphere, resulting in the

students' increased tolerance and ability to deal with the societal taboo, death. They are also exposed regularly to possibilities for personal growth and maturity as an essential part of the recovery process.
Session Eleven.   Theorists and researchers have noted the potential for growth and not merely the threat to well-being presented by traumatic stress.[11] Building on past material and previous interventions, this session focuses on ideas for rechanneling the students' energy. Questions like "What can you do with some of your time and energy that would make you feel better about this loss?" generate introspection and speculation by members. In addition, it is helpful for students to plan activities to "balance the ledger." For example, Karen and Jenny both decided to apply for peer-counseling training, recognizing that they could work especially well with other bereaved students. Owen was inspired to write a poem about his grief and newfound self-awareness. One group decided to plant a dogwood tree on the school grounds.

At some point during the school year, each group has been invited to share grief and growth experiences with other students. These field trips always provide the opportunities to interact with strangers on a very personal level. In this eleventh session, it is important for students to recognize these sharing and educating experiences as one indication that the grief experience has been a catalyst for growth.

Termination Phase

Session Twelve.   In preparation for termination, the twelfth session is spent enumerating and evaluating the group's accomplishments and shortcomings, discussing posttermination follow-up for individual members, and planning a celebration. During this pretermination session, it is anticipated that feelings of loss and abandonment from other life experiences may be reactivated. Keeping in mind this population's hypersensitivity to loss and termination, the leaders label and acknowledge these feelings. It is also pertinent to reiterate the opportunities available for potential growth in anticipated life transitions.

The group's accomplishments and shortcomings may be examined in relation to their meaning for individual members, their meaning to the leaders, and their relation to the group's purposes and goals.[12] The material generated during this process can be connected to daily life functioning with such questions as, "What have you learned about living that will help you with your next loss?"

and "Have there been ways you have caused yourself extra pain throughout this ordeal?"

In this session, it is also useful to discuss options for members' continued growth and grief management. Some students may feel sated and terminate the group experience. Others may be referred for more intense individual and/or family therapy. Still others may opt to join the group when it reconvenes the following semester to ensure an ongoing peer-support group and a therapeutic environment for coping with grief in the school setting. These seasoned members provide validity for potential new members and act as catalysts and role models in the group. Not only does the group benefit from these experienced members' participation, but the individuals have an additional opportunity to reinforce and augment their grief management.

In keeping with the adolescent's penchant for celebrating, the students always suggest having a party. Planning this ritual for ending the group is an appropriate activity during this pretermination session. The students take responsibility for the planning and execution of the final session.

Session Thirteen.   Celebrating life is the theme of the final session. The students always assume the party will be light-spirited and fun, and they bring beverages and snacks to share. On one occasion, two homemade cakes were presented to the group. Allyson's chocolate-frosted cake bore the finger-drawn inscription, "Understanding." Angel's white frosting was decorated in blue, saying "Friends Help a Lot." A handmade card, presented to the leaders, said, "We had a lot of fun in the group. It helped us out a lot. Thank you very much. We hope to be in this group next year, if you have one. Once again, thank you for your help! Now we know how much friends can help!"

This sort of cue provides a perfect entree for the leaders to acknowledge the group's ending. Summary statements directed toward individual members can highlight each one's personal growth. In addition, it is important to emphasize that this formal ending does not necessarily coincide with the end of personal grieving. Students are encouraged to discuss with family and group members the value of continuing the group experience.

Conclusion

Because of the enthusiastic response to this grief group by participants, their parents and friends, and the school staff, it has become a standard offering at the school. The group experience provides adolescents with an opportunity to expand their repertoire of intellectual and emotional responses to loss. Learning to manage their grief helps students return to an optimal level of functioning, so they are able to say, as did Camus, "In the midst of winter, I finally learned that there was in me an invincible summer."[13]

Notes and References

1. M. E. Hartford, *Groups in Social Work* (New York: Columbia University Press, 1971), p. 76.

2. I. D. Yalom, *The Theory and Practice of Group Psychotherapy* (New York: Basic Books, 1970), p. 10.

3. Ibid.

4. L. H. Frears and J. M. Schneider, "Exploring Loss and Grief within a Holistic Framework," *Personnel and Guidance Journal,* 58 (February 1981), pp. 341-345.

5. D. Balk, "How Teenagers Cope with Sibling Death: Some Implications for School Counselors," *School Counselor,* 31 (November 1983), p. 155.

6. See J. Krementz, *How It Feels When a Parent Dies* (New York: Alfred A. Knopf, 1981).

7. E. Lindemann, "Symptomatology and Management of Acute Grief," *American Journal of Psychiatry,* 101 (1944), pp. 141-148.

8. Hartford, *Groups in Social Work.*

9. Ibid.

10. D. S. Davenport, "A Closer Look at the 'Healthy' Grieving Process," *Personnel and Guidance Journal,* 59 (February 1981), pp. 332-335; D. Balk, "Effects of Sibling Death on Teenagers," *Journal of School Health,* 53 (January 1983), pp. 14-18; and Balk, "How Teenagers Cope with Sibling Death."

11. B. A. Baldwin, "A Paradigm for the Classification of Emotional Crises: Implications for Crisis Intervention," *American Journal of Orthopsychiatry,* 48 (July 1978), pp. 538-551.

12. Hartford, *Groups in Social Work.*

13. A. Camus, as cited in M. J. Moffat, *In the Midst of Winter: Selections from the Literature of Mourning* (New York: Random House, 1982), p. xv.

Sharing the Secret:
Reaching Children of Alcoholics

Robin H. Aronow

MANY CHILDREN HARBOR the secret of parental alcoholism. Alcoholic families have strict rules about not discussing the drinking problem outside of the home or even among family members. Beneath the silent front, however, is a population of children who now are recognized to be "at risk." Research suggests that children of alcoholics are at risk in several respects: They are most likely to become alcoholics (due to a combination of genetic and environmental factors) or to marry alcoholics.[1] They are often the victims of child abuse and neglect.[2] They frequently experience learning, behavioral, and psychological disorders.[3] To deal with the turmoil and inconsistency at home, children of alcoholics develop survival skills that may become ineffective in adulthood, thus leading to depression, a poor self-image, and relationship difficulties.[4]

An estimated 7 million children under the age of 20 and many more millions of "adult children" have at least one alcoholic parent.[5] Yet these children comprise an underidentified and underserved population.[6] Their secrets often remain secret unless a parent enters a sophisticated treatment program, which also addresses the children's needs.

The alcoholic parent may have access to Alcoholics Anonymous, the spouse to Alanon, and the teenage child to Alateen, but there are few resources for children under the age of 13 whose parents are alcoholics. The elementary schools are excellent places to begin to identify and simply "reach" these children and to implement services for them. The author is a school-based social worker who has developed programs for elementary school children of alcoholics. This article discusses the characteristics of these children and the implementation of interventive programs, including staff support, techniques of identification, use of in-school groups, and obstacles to referrals for treatment outside of school.

Children of Alcoholics and Their Families

What most children of alcoholics have in common is a chaotic, unpredictable, inconsistent home life that centers around the alcoholic and his or her drinking. The family structure is a rigid one characterized by extreme denial. The family becomes a closed unit that has a secret it shares with few, if any, others.[7]

The effect on the children may vary based on a number of factors including present age of child, age of child when drinking began, sex of alcoholic parent, relationship with alcoholic parent when sober, relationship with nonalcoholic parent, presence of violence in the home, severity of marital discord, family's willingness to seek help, and child's ability to develop relationships outside the home. Children of alcoholics grow up with feelings of shame, insecurity, fear, anger, hatred, guilt, and blame.

To cope with the turmoil at home, children of alcoholics develop skills that help them survive but may be detrimental to long-term functioning. Wegscheider discussed four survival types.[8] The first is the "Family Hero" or "Superkid," usually the oldest, who becomes overly responsible and overachieving. Second is the "Lost Child" who tends to be a loner—quiet, shy, and often ignored. Third is the "Mascot" or "Family Clown" who is cute and immature and will do anything for a laugh or attention. This child may have a learning disability or be hyperactive. Last is the "Scapegoat" or "Problem Child" who is hostile, defiant and draws negative attention. Each of the roles serves a purpose within the family and children may exhibit overlapping roles. Underneath each role there are feelings of hurt, inadequacy, rejection, and lack of trust that follow the child through life unless interventions occur.

Many young children of alcoholics will make their needs known, if only indirectly, by exhibiting learning and behavioral problems in school. These children are likely to be referred to the school social worker or psychologist to determine what is wrong. The school social worker also has an excellent opportunity to intervene on behalf of the Superkids and Lost Children—who are hurting as much, but tend to be overlooked in schools—if these children can be identified and brought to the worker's attention.

Implementing Programs

Programs can be implemented for children of alcoholics from within the schools as well as by using the schools as referral sources for outside programs. Model progams that are formally organized and staffed by both professionals and peer counselors are being developed around the country. Two such programs are CASPAR Decisions about Drinking (Cambridge and Somerville [Massachusetts] Program of Alcoholism Rehabilitation), and the Westchester County (New York) Student Assistance Program.[9] Even if such formal programs cannot be adopted, services for children of alcoholics can still be implemented using a school's own staff and inexpensive outside resources. What follows is a description of services within the school that the author provides as the only social worker covering 2,600 students.

The author is a substance abuse prevention worker in a school district that receives funding from the Nassau County Department of Drug and Alcohol Addiction, which in turn receives funding from the New York State Division of Substance Abuse Services. The author has the advantage of working for a school district that already accepts the concept of prevention and intervention services in regard to drug and alcohol addiction. In addition to providing social work services, the district also makes use of a science/health curriculum that contains a drug and alcohol education segment. In the sixth grade, a special program called "The Alcohol Valuing Project" is used by all teachers who have received special training. This is a combination values clarification and alcohol education program that specifically discusses family alcoholism.[10]

The above is noted because, before the needs of children of alcoholics can be addressed, several conditions must exist. First, drug and alcohol prevention must be seen as an important issue for elementary schools, and there must be a willingness to provide alcohol education, including a segment on family alcoholism. Many children of alcoholics are reached only by these class sessions in which learning facts about alcoholism may relieve them of their guilt, help them to understand what happens at home, show them they are not alone, and give them an opportunity to approach a teacher after class.

If a district does not have an alcohol education program, social workers can help by making school boards, administrators, and communities aware of the need for such a curriculum and by helping to choose an appropriate curriculum through, for example, a state alcoholism agency. They can also locate resources in the community such as speakers who can address classes on the subject.[11]

Second, the social worker must gain the support of the school staff to deal specifically with children of alcoholics. Staff are often resistant to dealing with "loaded" issues in the schools and may see children of alcoholics as a family problem with which the school has no business interfering. Staff may also feel uncomfortable dealing with children of alcoholics because of their own family experiences or attitudes toward alcohol.

The social worker should first discuss ideas with administrators and influential and sensitive teachers in each school. Justification for dealing with this population should be given and ways of reaching students should be explored. Soliciting staff input is essential for developing successful programs.

Once staff backing is acquired, in-service training is necessary. The social worker can either provide such training or arrange for outside alcoholism agencies to do it. In-service training will be discussed in more detail in the next section.

The last aspect, and perhaps the most important, is that social workers must receive their own alcoholism training. To be helpful to children of alcoholics, it is important for the worker to be sensitive to this special influence in a child's life. Too often in counseling, children are not asked if alcoholism plays a part in their lives or indications that it does are ignored. Generally this is because of the worker's own lack of knowledge or discomfort. The worker should take advantage of training given by local agencies as well as the numerous books and articles written on the topic.[12] In addition, it is recommended that the social worker "hook up" with a child specialist in family alcoholism with whom the worker can consult and commiserate. Working with children of alcoholics can be emotionally draining.

Techniques for Identification and Referral

Some children of alcoholics will never reach a social worker; they will never identify themselves to anyone. They have learned well the family rules: "Don't talk, don't trust, don't feel."[13] However, many children will come forward if they are made to feel safe and normal. Some children may feel ready to share their secret with their teacher, especially after a chaotic night at home or an alcohol education class. Others may give clues in class. A teacher who has received in-service training will know how to interpret these clues and be better prepared to deal with what the child shares or what is observed.

The author conducts in-service training programs. Sessions begin by showing a movie about children of alcoholics; the author uses *Soft Is the Heart of a Child* because it addresses the child's life in school.[14] After the film, reactions are solicited and facts about alcohol, alcoholism, and the effect on the child are discussed.

Each teacher is given a copy of the checklist, "Indications that a Child May Be Living with Family Alcoholism."[15] The indications are divided into two lists: "General Indications" include Monday morning tardiness, constant concern with getting home promptly, and extreme fear of having parents contacted; "Indications during Alcohol Education Activities" include a normally active child who becomes quiet, or vice versa, and an inability to think of healthy styles of drinking. As Deutsch noted, these behaviors may be related to other issues, but if patterns develop and there are other indications present, it is important for staff to consider the possibility of parental alcoholism.[16] Staff also are given an annotated bibliography of books to use with children of alcoholics, as well as the Johns Hopkins University questionnaire, "Are You an Alcoholic?" and a summary of family roles.[17]

The worker then explains how special the teacher's role is in identifying these children and how the teacher can provide the opportunity for a troubled child to share a secret. The teacher merely needs to ask a troubled child if things are all right at home, comment on observed behaviors during alcohol education sessions or changes in the child's behavior, listen without making judgments when a child talks, and/or attempt to get the child to speak with the school social worker. Sessions are concluded by letting teachers know that the worker is available to any of them to consult on cases, accept referrals, or help them with their own family problems.

In addition to in-service training, the author also speaks to PTA groups about services and writes articles in school newsletters to attract parental interest and referrals. The author uses a personal approach in identifying children of alcoholics and obtaining self-referrals. At the beginning of each school term, the author introduces herself in every fourth-, fifth-, and sixth-grade class. The children are asked if anyone knows what a social worker does.

Inevitably someone answers, "Helps with problems." They are asked if there is anyone who has *never* had a problem and, as no one raises a hand, the children see that there is nothing to be ashamed of in admitting to having a problem. The worker mentions that he or she has also had problems; some could be handled alone, but for others it was nice to have someone with whom to talk. It is explained that the worker is one person children can talk to if something is worrying them. The worker then asks what types of problems children might have. The author works with children who have a variety of problems, but to reach children of alcoholics, it is important to make a full list because they will often admit to a disguised or secondary problem until they learn to trust.

Answers are solicited from the children and divided into four categories. The first group is "family related" and includes parental fighting, divorce and remarriage, not getting along with parents, having too many responsibilities, dreaded brothers and sisters, illness or death in the family, financial problems, child abuse and neglect, and parents who drink too much or use drugs. These last two categories of problems are discussed in more detail to give the message that it is not the child's fault, and there are other children in school in the same situation. For that reason, the worker has put together a special private group the child may want to join.

The worker also shows the children a book called *Living with a Parent Who Drinks Too Much* and tells them that anyone can borrow it, even to write a book report.[18] Many children do borrow the book and some use it for reports; it is one of the best ways of identifying children of alcoholics, who may open up on their own or with gentle probing.

The second group of problems is "school related" and includes not working up to ability, difficulty concentrating on school work or homework, difficulty getting along with classmates or teachers, or always getting into trouble. Again these behaviors may be related to many other issues, but they also may be related specifically to being the child of an alcoholic.

The third group of problems is "peer related" and includes such problems as being a loner or left out; being too busy for friends; or being teased, bullied, or pressured by peers. The last group is called "How I Feel about Myself Problems." The worker talks about what it is like to feel down, sad, scared, and bad a lot of the time.

The children of alcoholics thus have many opportunities to relate to the issues discussed. The children are told they can come by themselves or in groups, or that their teachers or parents can refer them. They are reminded that their teacher is a good person to talk with but that the social worker is also there. The worker also gives assurances of privacy (unless the worker feels that the child is in a dangerous physical or emotional situation). The children are told that the first time they come no one needs to know, but after that parental permission (a district policy) is necessary. This is acknowledged to be a problem in working with children of alcoholics in the schools.[19] However, the worker also tells the children that fears about getting parental permission should not stop them from coming the first time and that the worker will help the child obtain permission. Only one parent's permission is required.

The worker concludes by telling the children they can stop by just to chat or say hello. Many children request to see the worker as the result of such a presentation, either shortly afterward or a long time later. Some are curious, some have small problems, and some continue on a regular basis. Many turn out to be children of alcoholics.

Interventions by the School Social Worker

The social worker meets with all children who are referred or who refer themselves because of concern about family alcoholism in order to assess the nature of the problem and the child's understanding of the alcoholism. It is necessary to determine whether the child's needs can be met within a school intervention program or if more intensive therapeutic services are indicated. The "Children of Alcoholics Screen Test" often is used.[20] A family genogram also is done with each child to diagram family relationships, trace alcoholism through the generations, and get the child's description of each family member in a nonthreatening way.

In addition, the worker meets with at least one parent to get another perspective of the home situation and to learn if anyone is involved in treatment or a self-help group. Possible services both in and out of school are discussed with both child and parent and recommendations are made. Both the alcoholic and the spouse are encouraged to seek help (see the later section on "Referrals to Outside Agencies"), and it generally is recommended that the child join an in-school group or some other form of group or family therapy. Groups are strongly recommended to help break the social isolation felt by children of alcoholics.[21] Most children join the groups but some opt to see the worker individually. The goal of all interventions is to help the children begin to talk, trust, feel, and have fun, and not just survive.

In-School Groups

Children of any age and both sexes join the same groups. Children with daily drinking, binge drinking, and recovering alcoholic parents join together. The groups have both educational and therapeutic components. They become safe places to learn about alcohol and alcoholism, share painful feelings about common experiences with "normal" schoolmates, provide and receive support, develop coping skills, and just act like children. The goal is prevention even if the parents never enter treatment.

A group starts at the beginning of each year although children may join any time during the term. Some children rejoin each year. Others terminate when they feel that they have gotten what they needed from the group.

Despite the comings and goings, the group tends to have a certain process. The first group session is a surprise for any child. One of the advantages of having a group in school is that children know one another or have seen each other. They walk in and say, "You?" and think to themselves, "That kid is normal." It is the first sign of relief. The leader is initially active as the children are not ready to expose themselves. The children are asked to introduce themselves and the leader discusses the purpose of the group in relation to family alcoholism, but the children are not asked to disclose anything about their families until they are ready to do so. The leader discusses group rules, which include no aggression and no put-downs, and gives special attention to discussing the confidentiality of group members and what is said. Members are given permission to discuss what they have said with their parents. They are told not to discuss the group with anyone else. Privacy is one of the biggest issues.

In the next few sessions the group begins to learn facts about alcohol and alcoholism. The disease concept is explained, myths are dispelled, and children learn that they are not to blame no matter what they have been told or previously believed. Books such as *Alcohol, What It Is, What It Does,* filmstrips, and games such as "concentration," in which children match up words and give definitions, are all helpful in the learning process.[22] During the next few weeks, the children begin to open up and share experiences and feelings, often for the first time. They look at their roles in the family and in the group. Groups have their share of members who enact each role. They begin to learn that they do not have to keep their roles.

Various activities are used to help children express their feelings. *My Dad Loves Me, My Dad Has a Disease* is a favorite book for drawing pictures that depict feelings.[23] Children also play the "Children of Alcoholics Using Self-Expression" game, put on masks of feelings, role-play, use puppets, complete sentences, and watch films.[24] The group often has parties to celebrate birthdays and holidays because these children usually do not have parties at home.

Many themes discussed by Morehouse become apparent.[25] These include the child's feeling responsible for a parent's drinking, equating a parent's drinking with not being loved, being disappointed by broken promises and hurt by name-calling, feeling powerless to stop the drinking, fearing the alcoholic will get hurt or sick, being confused by "wet' and "dry" behavior, finding it hard to bring friends home, and feeling angry not only at the alcoholic but also at the nonalcoholic parent for not making home life better.

After the children have gained a better understanding of their parents' alcoholism, the leader talks about what the children can do for themselves. The group talks about fun things each member can do instead of taking on adultlike responsibilities all the time. The importance of friends is emphasized. But the group also discusses practical solutions for problems when things are bad at home.

Teachers and parents report positive results from the groups. The withdrawn child comes out, the superkid relaxes, the clown settles down, and the scapegoat seeks positive attention. A real camaraderie develops between children who never had friends before. The members refer peers and siblings. Their high investment in the group is seen in giving up their recess time for meetings.

Referrals to Outside Agencies

Perhaps the hardest role of any school social worker is getting families to accept referrals for therapy outside of school. Accomplishing a successful referral for a family troubled by alcoholism to seek treatment is the greatest challenge. The worker must be prepared for more than a one-shot referral. It may take many sessions before the alcoholic and/or nonalcoholic parent will trust the worker and get past denial. The worker must realize that fear predominates: fear of revealing themselves, fear of giving up drinking without replacement, and fear of a change in self and family.[26]

In some cases, it may be best not to attack the defenses during the referral process and, instead, to refer the family on the basis of the child's behavior. Once in treatment, the therapist can begin to deal with the denial. However, it is usually best to engage both parents (unless it is a threat to the child to include the alcoholic parent) about the alcoholism. It is important to emphasize the child's love for them, as well as a knowledge of their concerns for their child and their strengths as parents. They must also be told that their child worries about them and that alcoholism is affecting the child's life and their lives in negative ways. Parents may also need alcohol education and that may be a less threatening initial referral than treatment. In extreme cases, protective services may have to be called. If the worker has the time and the patience, however, the family may be motivated toward seeking help.

The worker should have a reliable, competent contact person who can be called for an appointment even while the family is in the worker's office. A contact person should be established at Alcoholics Anonymous, Alanon, and an agency that specializes in families with alcoholism problems.

Summary

The difficulties that children of alcoholics exhibit in childhood and into adulthood now are being documented. Prevention programs offer promise in breaking the syndrome. The school social worker can play a critical role in these children's lives by helping to identify them, providing counseling, leading psychoeducational groups, and making referrals to outside agencies for all family members. Even if a child of an alcoholic never is identified, the social worker can help staff teach all students about alcohol and its effect on families. The child of an alcoholic may then be reached if only to learn that he or she is not alone and is all right.

Notes and References

1. See N. Cotton, "The Familial Incidence of Alcoholism: A Review," *Journal of Studies on Alcohol,* 40 (January 1979), pp. 89–116; and D. Goodwin, "The Genetics of Alcoholism: A State of the Art Review," *Alcohol Health and Research World,* 2 (Spring 1978), pp. 2–12.

2. See P. Diaz, "Child Abuse Reporting: A Major Issue for Young COAs," *The National Association of Children of Alcoholics Network,* 1 (Summer 1984), p. 5; and M. Hindman, "Child Abuse Projects Reveal Need for Treatment," *Alcohol Health and Research World,* 8 (Summer 1984), pp. 7, 13, 37.

3. See, for example, D. Cartwell, "Psychiatric Illness in the Families of Hyperactive Children," *Archives of General Psychiatry,* 27 (September 1972), pp. 414–417; M. Chafetz, H. Blane, and M. Hill, "Children of Alcoholics:

Observations in a Child Guidance Clinic," *Quarterly Journal of Studies on Alcohol,* 32 (September 1971), pp. 687–698; R. M. Cork, *The Forgotten Children* (Toronto, Ont., Canada: Alcohol and Drug Addiction Research Foundation, 1969); and N. el-Guelaly and D. Offord, "On Being the Offspring of an Alcoholic: An Update," *Alcoholism,* 3 (April 1979), pp. 148–157.

4. For this area as well as more information on the previously discussed risk factors, see R. Ackerman, *Children of Alcoholics: A Guidebook for Educators, Therapists and Parents* (Holmes Beach, Fla.: Learning Publications, 1983); C. Black, *It Will Never Happen to Me* (Denver, Colo.: M.A.C. Printing and Publications, 1982); C. Deutsch, *Broken Bottle, Broken Dreams: Understanding and Helping the Children of Alcoholics* (New York: Teachers College Press, 1982); and "Charter Statement," National Association for Children of Alcoholics, South Laguna, Calif., 1983.

5. M. Hindman and J. Small, "Children of Alcoholics: An Interview with the NIAAA Director," *Alcohol Health and Research World,* 8 (Summer 1984), pp. 3–5.

6. Booz-Allen and Hamilton, Inc., *An Assessment of the Needs of and Resources for Children of Alcoholic Parents* (Rockville, Md.: National Institute of Alcohol Abuse and Alcoholism, 1974).

7. This section is based on the works of Ackerman, *Children of Alcoholics;* Black, *It Will Never Happen to Me;* Cork, *The Forgotten Children;* and Deutsch, *Broken Bottles, Broken Dreams.*

8. S. Wegscheider, "Children of Alcoholics Caught in a Family Trap," *Focus on Alcohol and Drug Issues,* 2 (May–June 1979), p. 8.

9. Deutsch, *Broken Bottles, Broken Dreams,* pp. 163–177, 200–201.

10. *Alcohol Valuing Project* (New York: Nassau County Department of Drug and Alcohol Addiction, 1984).

11. Ackerman, *Children of Alcoholics,* pp. 201–207; and Deutsch, *Broken Bottles, Broken Dreams,* pp. 197–201.

12. Ibid. See also R. Ackerman, *Children of Alcoholics: A Bibliography and Resource Guide* (Indiana, Pa.: Addiction Research Press, 1984).

13. Black, *It Will Never Happen to Me.*

14. *Soft Is the Heart of a Child* (Skokie, Ill.: Gerald T. Rogers Productions).

15. Deutsch, *Broken Bottles, Broken Dreams,* pp. 195–196.

16. Ibid.

17. See R. Aronow, "Children of Alcoholics: An Annotated Bibliography and Resource Guide" (East Meadow, N.Y.: East Meadow School District, 1984). (Photocopied.)

18. J. Seixas, *Living with a Parent Who Drinks Too Much* (New York: Greenwillow Books, 1979).

19. L. DiCicco et al., "Recruiting Children from Alcoholic Families into a Peer Education Program," *Alcoholic Health and Research World,* 8 (Winter 1984), pp. 28–34.

20. J. Jones, *Children of Alcoholics Screen Test* (Chicago: Family Recovery Press, 1982).

21. See K. A. Brown and J. Sunshine, "Group Treatment of Children from Alcoholic Families," *Social Work with Groups,* 5 (Spring 1982), pp. 65–72; J. Deckman and B. Downs, "A Group Treatment Approach for Adolescent Children of Alcoholic Families," *Social Work with Groups,* 5 (Spring 1982), pp. 73–77; L. DiCicco et al., "Group Experiences for Children of Alcoholics," *Alcohol Health and Research World,* 8 (Summer 1984), pp. 20–24; E. R. Morehouse, "Working in the Schools with Children of Alcoholic Parents," *Health and Social Work,* 4 (November 1979), pp. 144–162; and S. Owen, J. Rosenberg, and D. Barkley, "Bottled Up Children: A Group Treatment Approach for Children of Alcoholics," *Group,* 9 (Fall 1985), pp. 31–42.

22. J. Seixas, *Alcohol, What It Is, What It Does* (New York: Greenwillow Books, 1977); and S. Nicholson, "Pre-schoolers from Chemically Dependent Families," *Focus on Family and Chemical Dependency,* 6 (September 1983), pp. 16–17.

23. C. Black, *My Dad Loves Me, My Dad Has a Disease* (Newport Beach, Calif.: ACT, 1979).

24. "C.A.U.S.E." game is available from the National Council on Alcoholism, Central Mississippi Area, Jackson; and J. Lemanczyk, "Getting Very Young COAs Off Their Rollercoaster," paper presented at Nassau County Showcase: Children of Alcoholics Conference, Uniondale, N.Y., January 1984 (photocopied).

25. Morehouse, "Working in the Schools with Children of Alcoholic Parents."

26. A. Petropoulos, "Intake and Referral in an Alcoholism Agency," *Social Casework,* 59 (January 1978), pp. 21–28.

Parent-Child Centers: A Preventive Service in a Multicultural Community

Gregory Grande
Antonio Gambini

THIS ARTICLE DESCRIBES the steps and processes in establishing a new service, a Parent-Child Center, within the school system; utilizing a multimethod approach that included community organization, group work, and informal counseling and referral; integrating social work and educational theories; and, subsequently, developing skills and programs that benefited the school, the students, the families, and the community. The preventive aspect of the program as well as the multicultural context are also addressed. This program is equally applicable to the native-born as well as to multicultural groups.

Background

The Good Beginnings Conference—conducted by the Toronto Board of Education in 1979 to commemorate the International Year of the Child—emphasized the need for a good start in life for children. A major theme of the conference was the need of some parents for programs on parenting and its many tasks.[1] A burgeoning of literature and experiments arising in the United States in the 1960s had focused on self-help networks to mobilize and help the poor and minorities. The literature also recommended that Parent-Child centers be organized and established on the grounds that these centers could play a major role in bringing children of the persistently poor "into the mainstream of our society within a generation."[2]

Child rearing had become increasingly difficult for many families. This was the result of changes in family and social structures, such as the scattering of the extended family, the disintegration of the neighborhood, the changes in role functioning between husband and wife, and the increase in single-parent families.[3] It was recognized that a child's early years of development have a significant impact on his or her future as a competent adult.

Urban Setting for Parent-Child Centers

In large cities, neighborhoods have become, to different degrees, more impersonal, removing supports from their residents. This is quite evident for mothers who remain at home to care for their children, particularly mothers in low-income and immigrant families, since their economic and social resources are limited. Mothers from these groups become isolated, lacking the mobility to see relatives and the few friends they may have, who often live in other parts of the city. Isolation can lead to the mothers' depression which, in turn, affects the children, particularly those of pre-school age, for whom the mother is usually the main source of social and intellectual stimulation. In a multicultural city such as Toronto, such problems are compounded by the parents' inability to understand English as well as cultural differences of a more subtle kind.[4]

Gordon indicated that a considerable number of children from families of low socioeconomic status lack the basic requirements for their physical well-being, with inadequate nutrition, health problems, and emotional difficulties being more prevalent than in families from a higher status.[5] Furthermore, parents of low socioeconomic status talk less with their children, affording them fewer opportunities to develop the cognitive skills necessary for the development of competence with language and numbers.

Parenting, a difficult task for most new mothers, is made harder for those who did not succeed in school and are unable to read well, who do not have the opportunity and the capacity to follow current child development findings, and who are afflicted by the many stresses caused by poverty, inadequate housing, and inadequate health information and services.[6] Traditionally, identified problems have been addressed through counseling, consisting of office interviews or home visits. This method, although successful with certain individuals, has been to some degree unsuccessful with working-class families. The lack of resources in the home, such as appropriate space and material; the difficulty for some parents of putting theoretical suggestions into practice; or possibly an underlying implication that intervention means they are incompetent may prevent counseling from being successful with some parents.

Furthermore, with continuous governmental cutbacks in social services and increasing caseloads, a group approach that emphasizes self-help and the establishment of neighborhood support systems is congruent with the changing focus of school social work.[7] This change is recognized by many boards of education, including the Toronto board.

Problem Identification

In September 1980, the strains of parenting became evident to two elementary school principals and a school social worker when they reviewed the previous years' social work cases. The principals, the school social worker, and some parents decided to establish two Parent-Child Centers as a way to meet the needs of children and parents.

Both schools were multiethnic. In one, the student body was composed of children of West Indian (40 percent), Portuguese (10 percent), Italian (10 percent), and Canadian Anglo-Saxon (40 percent) origins.[8] The neighborhood itself had a mixed population ranging from professionals in one-family dwellings to single-parent families and other welfare recipients in multifamily units. The families of the other school were mainly Italian (30 percent) or Greek (20 percent). The other 50 percent were of West Indian, Portuguese, and Canadian Anglo-Saxon backgrounds.[9] Most children were from low-income working-class families or had single mothers.

In both schools, it had been observed that many of the children were experiencing difficulties adapting to the school system. Many of the families were recent immigrants, unfamiliar with Canadian customs. A considerable number of the mothers were isolated and needed the opportunity to make new friends and encouragement to learn a new language. Some of the women hoped to reenter the work force but lacked the self-confidence needed to acquire the necessary skills.

In both schools, many children attended as early as age 4; they came from homes where parents were frustrated and confused about parenting and child development. Some of the children were deprived of experiences that promote normal, healthy development and growth. The families and home environments were often unstable and unresourceful. The children lacked positive, enriching personal experiences and were rarely provided with sufficient cultural and intellectual stimulation. Their families were recent immigrants who were unfamiliar with the educational system and the school's expectations. For example, some had difficulties understanding the complementary roles of parent and teacher. Instead, they expected the school to be solely responsible for the child's education, with home and school as two basically unconnected environments. Also, their understanding of a school curriculum was based mainly on their own experiences in their country of origin, where activities such as cutting, pasting, and painting, which promote fine-motor skills and creativity, were not used in the classroom. Such activities were not seen as important. The children appeared to be lost between an unfamiliar, complex educational system and an uninformed, isolated, family support system.

Furthermore, some of the parents had difficulty in meeting the minimum standards of child management, for example, nutrition, clothing, and discipline. Some were single parents who were difficult to reach through regular existing channels.

Meetings between school personnel and community agencies resulted in a plan for a service that would attract parents of preschool children and allow them the opportunity to have supportive experiences with children's activities that would lead to their children's success in school. The service was to be adapted from Parent-Child Centers already established in the United States.

Goals and Objectives

The three main objectives of the Parent-Child Centers were: (1) to assist parents with parenting skills while increasing their awareness of child-rearing techniques; (2) to enrich the lives of preschoolers in the intellectual, social, physical, and recreational areas of their growth and development; and (3) to decrease the isolation of young mothers in the community and to increase their sense of self-worth. The general goals of the Parent-Child Centers in these two particular schools were the enhancement and growth of both children and parents through provision of specific services.[10]

To increase parents' awareness and knowledge of alternative parenting techniques, the following program was planned:

1. The enhancement of parent-child interaction by providing an opportunity for interaction and role modeling.

2. The improvement of parenting skills through formal and

informal discussions.[11] The formal discussions included workshops on parenting skills, nutrition, and child abuse. The informal discussions centered on appropriate child-management techniques. For example, the centers served nutritional snacks (celery sticks, oranges, apples, cheese, milk), thus exposing parents to alternatives to "junk food" while establishing and discussing better eating habits for children.

3. The opportunity for mothers to interact with one another and to make friends.

4. The increase of awareness and use of community resources through casual information-sharing, workshops, and outings.

5. The identification of children and families with problems requiring professional help and the making of appropriate referrals.

6. The increase of self-confidence in parenting through participation in the various activities.

7. The improvement of their language proficiency by being given the chance to attend English classes with free baby-sitting. This helped mothers to enhance their self-esteem and enabled them to use other child-focused community resources.[12]

Administration and Organizational Structure

Once the decision to establish the two Parent-Child Centers was made, it was agreed that the programs would be more effective if both users and staff were involved in the design and administration of the services. Participation was solicited from the parents by writing letters and by presenting the concept to the Parent-Teacher Association in each school. Some parents showed enthusiasm and immediately became involved. To maintain the parents' involvement in a significant way, it was agreed by the parents and professionals that the board of directors of the centers should be composed of a minimum of five parents and a maximum of four professionals. Most of the parents had never been involved in an organization and were reluctant to serve on a board of directors. The lack of experience of those who decided to be part of the board, combined with, in most cases, a lack of formal education and poor self-concept, caused them to be very dependent on the professionals for directions. As a result, even though the parents constituted the majority on the board of directors, decision making remained in the hands of the professionals. This problem was not helped by the fact that the school principals involved were not accustomed to dealing with parents as equals.

Parent development was an ongoing process since most parents remained involved in the board of directors for one to two years at the most. Regular parents' meetings were held at each center to discuss the type of programs parents found most beneficial so that the services provided by the centers did not remain static, but were constantly evolving.[13] The Parent-Child Centers became incorporated and held a monthly board of directors meeting. One staff member attended the meeting to give input from the staff. Each board had two subcommittees: program development and advertising and funding. Committee members acted as volunteers to assist in the administration of the centers. Task groups were also formed as the need arose. The subcommittees met each month to share information, to give support to the staff, to evaluate the program, and to share resources and ideas.[14]

Staff

Hancock states in her book: "School social workers, along with other staff, can work toward humanizing the school by creating a warmer, more personal climate for students and their families."[15] Each center employed two staff members with training in child development and educational theories, who were able to speak a second language such as Italian, Greek, or Spanish and to understand the culture of the clients and their family structure. The staff members' duties were to provide activities for the children and parents, to discuss concerns with individual parents, and to refer those parents who were in need to outside resources.[16] It should be stressed that many parents using the centers had been involved in the past with traditional agency-based services and had not found them beneficial. Consequently, a traditional therapeutic focus was avoided; self-help and group support was the preferred model. Referrals to other agencies were not suggested unless the child was in need of protection or the parent indicated that specialized help was wanted. Attached to the two centers was an outreach worker whose functions were to advertise the centers within the community and to become involved with severely disadvantaged and depressed parents not reached by agency-based services. A coordinator supervised the staff and the programs. The coordinator was directly responsible to the school social worker who, for economic reasons, acted as executive director. Supervision was given on a weekly basis. Regular evaluation sessions were held to assist staff and to assess the effectiveness of each of the centers.

The Social Work Services of the Toronto Board of Education sponsored the centers until incorporation was obtained. During the interim, the school social worker was also responsible for administrative details.

Program

The centers were open four days per week from 9:00 A.M. to 1:30 P.M. and one day per week from 9:00 A.M. TO 3:30 P.M. Most parents preferred the morning programs because most toddlers had a nap in the afternoon. The centers were also kept open on a trial basis for one evening per week from 5:00 P.M. to 8:00 P.M. for three months in order to determine whether working parents would use the services. The response to the evening program was minimal, and the practice was discontinued.

The activities of the centers provided preschool-age children with a variety of stimulating and positive experiences for the purpose of enhancing their physical, social, and cognitive development. Some were designed to improve gross-motor and fine-motor coordination through the use of large blocks, sandbox, Lego sets (educational construction toys, appropriate for improving fine-motor coordination, perceptual concepts, and so forth), puzzles, finger painting, water play, building materials, cutting and pasting, and simple crafts. Activities to improve verbal skills included reading stories, songs, and nursery rhymes. Talking to the children enriched their vocabulary during the other activities offered. Some activities gave the children sensory experiences, such as listening to music, playing musical instruments, touching various materials to compare textures, and tasting and smelling foods before and after cooking. The programs at the center also provided an opportunity for children to develop their social skills; the interaction with other children taught them cooperation and sharing through collective play in group situations.

The centers offered an environment for parents and preschool-age children to play, learn, and explore together. Parent-child interaction was enhanced by parents' involvement in activities with their children and by observation of interactions involving other parents and workers with the children. Parenting knowledge was expanded through informal discussions with other parents and the personnel at the centers and through workshops on various child-related subjects. The workshops were organized by the staff, but the topics were chosen by the parents. A common factor in the

Parent-Child Centers is that many mothers come to them because they feel isolated. A reward lies in sharing concerns with peers. Self-help groups were formed at the request of the mothers attending the centers. Topics of discussion varied; most common were child-rearing techniques, assertiveness, self-confidence, marital problems, and women's role in society. The centers increased the use of other community resources through casual information-sharing and printed material.

Most programs were presented informally. Parents had the choice of participating in the programs offered, of initiating an activity of their own, or of not participating. Each parent was responsible for his or her children unless the parent was involved in a discussion group, at which point the staff would care for the children.

Funding and Alternative Services

During their first year of operation, the Parent-Child Centers were funded through a grant from Canada Employment and Immigration (Canada Community Development Projects) and a grant from the Toronto Board of Education. In the second year of operation, grants were provided by the Ministry of Community and Social Services and by Metropolitan Toronto Social Services. Difficulties, however, were encountered continuously when efforts were made to obtain ongoing funding since Parent-Child Centers were neither counseling centers nor day care centers. The uncertainty related to funding created feelings of insecurity and frustration among the parents. Because the Parent-Child Centers had proved successful in terms of attendance and feedback, the Toronto Board of Education decided to provide ongoing funding through its Continuing Education Department.

There had been concern in Ontario, as elsewhere, about the cost of the traditional mode of intervention. The concern gave rise to a search for alternatives. The Ministry of Community and Social Services in Ontario was pursuing a policy of deinstitutionalization. A policy paper in the province of Ontario once again emphasized the responsibility of the family unit for meeting its basic needs with critical support given by the community.[17] The perceived gap between the poles of the traditional and newer modes of intervention indicated a need for informal social supports in the community. The Parent-Child Centers represented such an intervention. They emerged at a time when Family Court, Children's Aid Societies, and Public Health and Hospitals were looking for a resource to which they could refer clients who required both emotional support and child-rearing information, not necessarily therapeutic. This was also a time when professionals were looking for a consistent supportive service for adolescent parents. It had to be made clear to funding sources that the centers would produce positive results by involving parents who were experiencing difficulty in raising their children and who could make use of the supportive community that parents create for themselves at the centers. The centers were low-cost services because (1) they made use of available space such as unused school classrooms, (2) they provided an opportunity for parents to learn from one another, and (3) they helped to develop indigenous leadership.[18]

Outreach

Outreach was an important component of the Parent-Child Centers. It was an ongoing process that remained a major part of each worker's responsibility, acting with the "outreach/advertising subcommittee" in each center. A variety of methods were used, such as door-to-door canvassing in the school neighborhoods; distribution of a multilingual flyer to the private sector, institutions, and community centers; media coverage (e.g., *Toronto Star, Toronto Sun,* CFTR Radio, Global T.V.), including ethnic media; and a letter of announcement to related agencies and institutions with a follow-up visit by one worker from each center to describe the centers and to establish a referral network with the agency. A slide-tape presentation, prepared for major institutions and agencies, received an enthusiastic response. Some of the agencies were the Italian Immigrant Aid Society, Catholic Children's Aid and Metropolitan Children's Aid Societies, Toronto Western Hospital, Community Centers, Earlscourt Children's Home, and the Immigrant Women's Center. Responses were measurable by the increased number of referred cases from some of these agencies. Many found the concept to be new, yet one that would fill a long-standing need.[19]

Personal contact through door-to-door canvassing was the most successful method of outreach. It provided the most positive results by reaching and motivating isolated and depressed parents who were not in touch with other resources. The major function of the outreach worker was to make contact with such parents.

Evaluation

A formal written evaluation has yet to be done. However, quarterly evaluative reports and financial auditing were submitted to the funders. Regular meetings of parents and staff and the various subcommittees provide ongoing evaluation of the programs' relevance and effectiveness. The coordinator of the two centers and the school social worker—who acted as a "two-person executive committee"—prepared evaluative reports on staff performance and the effects of the programs on the users, the school, and the community.[20] The major outcomes of the programs were improved child-parent interaction; increased language development in children; improved home-school relationship; increased knowledge of good nutrition for the total family; increased parental and community participation in the school; enhanced communication in the family through improving the self-image of parents and children and demonstrating appropriate communication patterns; development of leadership and a self-help network. A further positive outcome was the higher credibility and visibility of the school social worker with school personnel, parents, and community agencies.

Conclusion

This article outlined the steps and processes for the establishment of Parent-Child Centers in two elementary schools in a multicultural community. It indicated the efforts to mobilize parents, schools, and community agencies around relevant areas and a "felt need" in the interests of instituting a preventive program both for preschoolers and parents. The positive results resolved the funding problem; the three-year project became an ongoing program of the Toronto Board of Education in the Continuing Education Department. This preventive service is pointing the way to creative and appropriate programs in the school that should continue so that the school can be seen as a community center with a therapeutic perspective. This article illustrated the expanded role of the school social worker in light of a declining enrollment, budgetary cutbacks, and limited resources. The development of self-help groups finds an appropriate locus in the school system, specifically in elementary school communities.

Notes and References

1. Good Beginning Conference sponsored by Board of Education, Toronto, Ont., Canada, October 1979.

2. J. M. Hunt, *The Challenge of Incompetence and Poverty: Papers on the Role of Early Education* (Urbana: University of Illinois Press, 1969), p. 223.

3. G. Grande and T. Gambini, "Report on Together Parent-Child Centers." Funding proposal submitted to Canada Employment and Immigration, October 1980, p. 1. (Photocopied.)

4. M. Linton, "Toronto, Kids' Beat," *Homemaker's Magazine* (November 1982), p. 126.

5. E. W. Gordon, "Parent/Child Centers: Their Basis in Behavioral and Educational Sciences," *American Journal of Orthopsychiatry*, 41 (January 1971), pp. 13–38.

6. B. Gross and R. Gross, "Parent-Child Development Centers: Creating Models for Parent Education," *Children Today*, 6 (November–December 1977), p. 19.

7. B. L. Hancock, *School Social Work* (Englewood Cliffs, N.J.: Prentice-Hall, 1982), p. 249.

8. "School Contracts 1980," Social Work Services, Board of Education, Toronto, Ont., Canada. (Photocopied.)

9. Ibid.

10. Grande and Gambini, "Report on Together Parent-Child Centers," p. 2.

11. M. Fine and C. Brownstein, "Parent Education and the School Social Worker," *Social Work in Education*, 6 (Fall 1983), pp. 44–45.

12. A. Gambini, R. Gaglione, and G. Grande, "Report on Together Parent-Child Centers," January 26, 1981 to May 30, 1981: Application for Further Funding," submitted to Canada Employment and Immigration, Toronto, June 1981.

13. Gambini, Gaglione, and Grande, "Report on Together Parent-Child Centers," June 1981, Appendix D, p. 11.

14. Ibid., p. 12.

15. Hancock, *School Social Work*, p. 17.

16. Gambini, Gaglione, and Grande, "Report on Together Parent-Child Centers," June 1981, p. 13.

17. M. Birch, "The Family as a Focus for Social Policy" (Toronto, Canada: Government of Ontario Report, May 1979). (Photocopied.)

18. Grande and Gambini, "Report on Together Parent-Child Centers," October 1980, p. 9.

19. Ibid., p. 8.

20. Gambini, Gaglione, and Grande, "Report on Together Parent-Child Centers," June 1981, p. 16.

Integration Is Not Enough

Gayle Twilbeck Wykle

IN THE 1955 *Brown v. Board of Education of Topeka* case, the Supreme Court ordered that all public schools be racially integrated "with all deliberate speed."[1] That decision marked a culmination of long years of struggle as much as it defined new lines of battle. The Federal District Courts, who were ordered to monitor the implementation of the decision, continue to this day to receive and reject desegregation plans that would have the intended or unintended effect of continuing *de facto*, albeit no longer *de jure*, racial segregation. At the beginning of each new decade after a significant event, we often pause to assess how far we have come. It is not only to take pride in our progress but to adjust, where necessary, for the work yet to be done.

It is disappointing that a policy decision holding such great promise has produced such mixed results in more than 30 years. "Indeed resistance has been so fierce that today there are more blacks attending all or predominantly black schools than was true in 1954 when *Brown I* was handed down."[2] Yet some black civil rights leaders contend that it was never school integration itself that was the goal, but the personal status and economic benefits to be derived from equality in education that were sought. Was integration the wrong goal?

The profession of social work is necessarily involved in the civil rights movement. As professional social workers in public education, we have a stake in school integration policy. We must review the events leading to the *Brown* decision; the course of its implementation to date, including relevant social and demographic changes; and the conflicting voices of black civil rights leaders if we are to achieve consistency in our actions and goals. We must be able to connect unfolding policy processes to specific actions in our daily practice if we are to enable clients to experience their own power to become an active force in determining how things will be in our schools.

"Separate but Equal" and the *Brown* Case

Prior to the *Brown* case, states were permitted, not required, to have segregation laws. In many states, many schools and other public facilities were integrated long before 1954. Where racially segregated facilities were maintained, "separate but equal" was the legal standard to be met. That doctrine was established in the 1896 *Plessy v. Ferguson* Supreme Court decision that public railroad car accommodations could be separate for black and white passengers if the accommodations were equal.[3] In the years that followed *Plessy*, the legality of "separate but equal" came into question in several cases regarding public facilities but was not attacked directly. Instead, progress in racial discrimination cases was made that prepared the way for *Brown* as the Court refined the "separate but equal" principle. One way the Court did this was by requiring an almost impossible-to-meet yardstick for equal facilities ("stone-for-stone, book-for-book").[4] Another way was by ordering black applicants to be admitted to white schools where no equivalent school for black students existed.[5]

In the 1930s, the newly created Legal Defense and Education Fund of the National Association for the Advancement of Colored People (NAACP) settled on public colleges and universities as the area in which to concentrate its efforts. Higher education, especially in the South, was more vulnerable to legal attack because few states had made even a pretense of providing separate public universities for black students.[6]

In the North, where blacks are less numerous and have been residentially concentrated in certain neighborhoods or ghettos, the policy of drawing school district lines around neighborhoods resulted in predominantly white or predominantly black schools. "Northern style" segregation seemed innocently the chance result of exercising free choice. In the South, where most black people live and are relatively dispersed among whites, segregation could not be maintained by neighborhood school boundaries. Instead, separate schools in the same neighborhood could be maintained only by force of law (*de jure*)—which very clearly denied individual choice.[7]

It was "Southern style" segregation by law that was most humiliating, easier to attack in the courts on Constitutional grounds, and easier to fight financially with the limited resources available to the Legal Defense and Educational Fund.[8] As stated by Carter, one of the lawyers who worked closely with Thurgood Marshall, Chief Counsel of the Legal Defense Fund, in representing the plaintiffs in the segregation cases:

> Removal of the barrier *Plessy* imposed was our first priority. As long as *Plessy* remained the national norm, the North could perpetuate its own myth that it was more advanced and progressive than the South in dealing with the racial question.
>
> *   *   *   *   *
>
> Accordingly, the basic postulate of our strategy and theory in *Brown* was that the elimination of enforced segregated education would necessarily result in equal education.[9]

Finally, in a bold move in the *Brown* case, the NAACP lawyers attacked the "separate but equal" doctrine directly and were successful; the Court concluded in 1954 that "separate educational facilities are inherently unequal" and that "segregation is a denial of the equal protection of the law."[10] The Court declared segregation illegal but did not spell out a remedy for the injustice. Instead, separate argument on an implementation plan was delayed until the following year when the Court ordered that schools be desegregated "with all deliberate speed."[11] The Court did not impose a deadline for school boards to submit acceptable plans, as requested by the federal government, or a deadline for the end of segregated schools, as requested by the NAACP lawyers.

Implementing *Brown*—The Early Years

For several years after the order to end segregation, most white people's energy in the South was invested in devising ways to avoid integrating schools. The principle established in *Brown* allowed black citizens to establish other areas of rights, such as equal access to public parks, restaurants, voter registration, and many others.[12] In the schools, progress has been slow. The first line of resistance by whites was in the Federal District Courts, which aided whites by interpreting the *Brown* decision to mean only that "The Constitution . . . does not require integration. It merely forbids discrimination."[13]

President Eisenhower did not use all the powers of the executive branch of government to enforce the law regarding integration. It was not until the brief Kennedy Administration that there was affirmative action to enforce the desegregation order. President Johnson continued efforts in the enforcement of *Brown* and was successful in obtaining new civil rights laws. Also, although President Kennedy had the opportunity to make two appointments to the Supreme Court, it was President Johnson, a Southerner, who appointed the first black justice, Thurgood Marshall, to serve on the nation's highest court.[14]

When the courts became firm in requiring desegregation, whites surrendered urban public schools to black students and retreated to private schools or to suburban areas, which they incorporated, including their own exclusive public school systems, under local control. That is, because of "white flight," Northern style segregation spread to the South and to other parts of the nation. The original problem had been desegregating black and white schools within a system, not desegregating entire white and black school systems—especially when those systems are separated by municipal and county boundaries demarcating separate geographic units of government and taxation. The force of court orders cannot so easily deal with urban whites who exercise their right to choose private schools nor can it be used to demand cooperation among school systems under separate local governments.

Without a direct legal assault on housing patterns, breaking up racially homogenous school districts within a system was achieved speedily only by court-ordered school reassignment and by busing. Because many children who are bused have long rides to schools—so distant and unfamiliar that parents cannot easily maintain supportive involvement in their child's education—this plan has been very unpopular with both black and white citizens. It had immediate results, but the gains were diminished as many black and many more white parents who had the financial means chose to send their children to private schools.

Efforts to deal with housing patterns were made in the legislature. In 1968 President Johnson was able to push through Congress the Fair Housing Act, which made it illegal to discriminate in any way in advertising, showing, renting, or selling real estate to anyone who can afford to pay the price.[15] However, the law cannot change housing patterns in one sweeping gesture. Because it requires many individual voluntary decisions to pay the price asked and to move where one may be socially rejected, the Fair Housing Act has not resulted in integrated neighborhoods that provide integrated public schools.

In a move that some hope will lure whites back to public schools in the cities, the Federal District Courts have recently looked favorably on desegregation plans that rely in part on "magnet" or "alternative" schools designed to offer special programs not always available in private schools. This plan has met with some success, but, like the housing law, it depends on voluntary individual actions.

Of the 45.2 million elementary and secondary school students enrolled in the fall of 1983, only 87.4 percent were in public schools—down from an 88.5 percent share in 1980.[16] Not only is the private school enrollment increasing, but the number of private schools is also increasing to meet the demand. Court-ordered integration, in the long run, has inadvertently provoked increased segregation.[17]

Implementing *Brown* Today

Many black civil rights leaders are so disillusioned by the failure of the court order to be as effective an instrument of change as expected and by the increasing intractability of the problem of achieving integrated schools in all communities that they are breaking the "unwritten civil rights Commandment: Thou shalt not publicly criticize."[18]

Some civil rights leaders are not sure that integration should ever have been a goal in the fight to end racial discrimination. There is fear that people may misinterpret it as a belief among black people that they cannot achieve a quality education unless they attend "white" schools.[19] To put that kind of speculation to rest, Sowell, a black economist, pointed out that many black students received a solid education at all-black schools before and after the *Brown* decision.[20]

The original theory of the lawyers arguing *Brown* was that eliminating segregation would necessarily result in equal education. Integration was to be used simply as a means to quality education through a share in the same school resources provided to white students. More than 30 years later, schools are not fully integrated. Black students now represent 80 percent or more of the public school population in many large cities. In some systems there are not enough white students remaining to be redistributed to achieve a racial balance, and further use of court-ordered busing or school reassignment will probably drive more students of both races to private schools. Schools are being resegregated—black systems in the cities, white systems in the suburbs.[21]

Some conclude that energy spent on integration is being wasted and should be redirected instead to the problem of providing a quality education to black students wherever they are—even in today's *de facto* segregated schools.[22] We cannot help but wonder whether this is a suggestion from black civil rights leaders that the "race problem" needs a little "benign neglect."[23] Indeed, this means settling for "separate but equal," but with a difference from the pre-*Brown* days. Now black citizens have a choice.

For those black students who do attend integrated schools, and therefore have the opportunity to benefit from the same school resources as whites, the research findings on results of that opportunity are mixed in terms of whether it is successful. However, disproportionately more black than white students fail grades, drop out, and do poorly on achievement tests.[24] Because neither integration nor a quality education for all black students has been achieved, there seems to be a questioning of the original goal and a search for new tactics.

Should there be an ever greater effort to achieve integration? The battle against today's widespread *de facto* segregation is more difficult than the one against *de jure* segregation. Should the interest in integration be abandoned or neglected in favor of quality education?

Indeed, there are two separate problems having different bases and different solutions. Both should be pursued with the same determination. Integration, insofar as it demonstrates freedom from racial discrimination, is a natural feature of a pluralistic society where all people are valued equally. Equal opportunities and equal rights cannot be realized until citizens know about and are prepared to use their opportunities and rights. That is one of the main goals of public education: to provide an informed citizenry who can act effectively in public and private matters.[25] Education, then, is to prepare citizens for all other rights and responsibilities, but it too requires some preparedness. What are the factors necessary to benefit from educational opportunity?

Social Work and School Integration

The profession of social work must respond to the issues outlined above regarding the current status of school integration and quality education equally available to students in public schools. The final section of our Code of Ethics makes it clear that we are responsible for working toward an integrated society.[26] It is difficult to imagine that without integrated schools. Do we clearly represent those values—pluralism and equal educational opportunity—in our daily practice?

It requires action both at a macro, or community, level and at a micro, or individual/family/group, level of practice. Community-level action is not a specialization that can be separated from direct services. It requires a clear understanding of goals and values and a personal commitment to inform oneself and one's clients of avenues of action. We do not live in a world totally shaped by others with whom we have no influence and by forces over which we have no control. Our clients will not trust our stated values and will continue to feel powerless themselves if we, as direct-service practitioners, do not act on our commitment to change the system where necessary. PTA meetings, state textbook committees, school board meetings, city and state government sessions, voter registration drives, and professional social work meetings all offer the opportunity for us to participate and to enable our clients to participate in shaping the world around us.

Integration and quality education, if we mean achievement, are related but different problems. Integration is a goal because without it there is no equality. Quality education does not depend only on school integration. Many students in all-black schools do achieve. Programs such as magnet and alternative school plans have been successful in drawing students voluntarily into programs that are integrated, quality education programs.

A striking feature of all efforts of the civil rights leaders to obtain quality education for all has been the meticulous avoidance of any discussion of individual responsibility in education. There is great difficulty in destroying the myth that black people are incapable of learning very much.[27] Therefore, it is not difficult to understand a fear that when more black than white children fail, admission of any personal responsibility in school failure may be misinterpreted as evidence that the myth is correct. Indeed there is that risk. Similar to the concern about integration as the goal of the civil rights movement is the concern that the desire for integration may be misinterpreted as wanting to be with one's "betters." The problem regarding quality education is one of either-or thinking. That is, either the failure of black children to learn is the fault of the system or is the fault of the individual—but not both. The fear is that to admit any individual responsibility may lead to the conclusion that failure to achieve is due only to individual factors.

The problem of blaming the individual versus the system is one that has been recognized and discussed in social work.[28] It has also been recognized by black social scientists with regard to black students' disproportionate failure to achieve in school.[29] This insistence on blaming only the system in order to avoid possible misunderstanding is not worth the cost to black students who are being deprived of all that they need for academic achievement. Black students and parents are encouraged to view failure to achieve as evidence that teachers, school systems, or tests are racially discriminatory. By implication, any willingness to take responsibility for learning, such as an admission of a lack of interest, a lack of preparation, or the lack of support from home necessary for attendance, is discouraged.

The insistence on blaming only the system encourages thinking that only the system needs to be changed to produce academic achievement because the system alone is at fault. Indeed, the need for system change is vast, and no one should minimize the need. However, this kind of thinking is a distortion of the educational process. Teachers can only teach; students must do the learning. Schools define what must be taught in what amount of time. Teachers present information and tasks designed to enable students to reach learning goals, and they present tests designed to measure students' progress toward the stated goals. It is not clear how much we expect teachers to motivate students, and some teachers are more inspirational than others. However, whatever its source, at some point enough motivation must come from students to engage themselves in learning.[30] Learning is the responsibility of the student, not the teacher. Learning is separate from teaching and occurs only if the student wants to learn. Similar to therapy with clients, treatment activities of the therapist are useless unless the clients engage themselves in the process. The insistence on blaming the system discourages us from looking at individual and family factors related to learning.

If only the system is to blame, then a nonracist system will result in high achievement rates for black children. They, like their white classmates, should move through the system to graduation.

So goes the reasoning. Prevented from admitting the great personal and family needs of black children for assistance to learn, school personnel have been reluctant to offer help because it would mean that the individual and family, not just the system, need some adjustment if learning is to occur. Educators are caught in the dilemma of not being able to meet recognized needs of black schoolchildren who fail in great numbers yet having to produce evidence of achievement such as passing grades and graduation. The only acceptable response to fulfill both conditions of the dilemma has been social promotion to create the illusion of achievement or setting teacher and school demands so low that students do pass the tests given. Students are not told that they are socially promoted or that the work presented to them is far below grade level and is lowered to whatever they can pass.[31] Teachers and schools want to avoid being called racist, and they want students to have the boost to self-esteem and personal identity that comes with the experience of success. When the students and parents do learn about the lie, they are discouraged from facing it. Is this illusion of achievement—this lie—an improvement over the racist lie of racial inferiority?

Today's achievement lie requires that we pretend black people are educated even when they are not. The racist lie demanded that we pretend black people were ignorant when they were not. Today's lie of unearned diplomas and certificates—at least not earned at the standard level of tasks—is just as cruel as the racist lie. At what point does anyone, black or white, become aware of the lie? And what is the remedy for students who have a college or graduate degree, are barely functionally literate, and cannot perform employment tasks at a level at which the diploma certifies that they should be able to perform? "Social promotions" in employment? Indeed, we have it. The lie requires it.

As social workers, we cannot participate in this duplicity. If we are to honor the ethic of self-determination for our clients, then they need full information. That begins with honest feedback in evaluations of their performance and discussion of factors over which they have control in the learning process. Assistance cannot be provided in a way that casts blame, but in a way that enables. It is clients' right and our duty.

Social workers are the only school personnel specifically trained to deal with the family as the sponsor of the child in school. Today there is increased interest in the role of parents in the educational process. The door is open in those states that have school social workers. Efforts must not be limited to direct services to individual students but must extend to school system and community involvement to interpret what is involved in families sponsoring children in school.[32] Further efforts are needed to educate states that do not have school social workers in their need for assistance with the task of developing a new, more involved partnership with parents.

Conclusions

In more than 30 years since *Brown*, we have removed the burden of racial segregation *de jure* in the schools. Despite the continued experience of what Lightfoot, a black civil rights leader, described as "the subtle exclusion and microaggressions that I experience daily in my almost all-white...middle class school,"[33] there has been immeasurable progress in civil rights. The principle established in *Brown* was applied in subsequent cases, regarding employment, entertainment, voting, and many other rights, to remove racial barriers. The fact that there is much to be done, still against some resistance, cannot cause us to belittle our progress.

The fact that removing Southern style segregation *de jure* has not been easy and has resulted in Northern style *de facto* segregation does not mean that integration cannot be achieved or should be abandoned as a goal. In the words of Judge Carter, one of the leading attorneys for the plaintiffs in *Brown*, who is weary but will not abandon hope, "Integrated education must not be lost as the ultimate solution."[34] As social workers, we can do no less. However, social work is at odds with the civil rights leaders who persist in blaming and demanding changes only in the system without attention to how this one-sided approach affects the learning process.

Integration is not enough. What is needed are more changes in the system as well as attention to individual factors in learning. Failure to admit learning difficulties, coupled with the need to produce instant success, has led to the achievement lie. The effort to produce high school and college graduates among students who have great learning disadvantages, with no remedial assistance, led to social promotions and unearned diplomas. The lie continued into employment. Participation in the lie is contrary to social work ethics and prevents social workers from delivering services that they are uniquely qualified to deliver and that would enable black students to learn to change the system on their own. Only when both integration (and other system factors) as well as individual factors in learning are addressed will social work fulfill its commitment to clients' public schools.

Notes and References

1. Brown v. Board of Education of Topeka, 347 U.S. 483 (1954) and 349 U.S. 294 (1955). Although the Court declared segregation illegal in 1954, the case was scheduled the following year for argument on implementation of a desegregation order. Because the case was heard in two parts, it is often referred to as Brown I and Brown II.

2. R. L. Carter, "A Reassessment of Brown v. Board," in D. Bell, ed., *Shades of Brown* (New York: Columbia Teachers College, 1980), p. 25.

3. Plessy v. Ferguson, 163 U.S. 537 (1896).

4. Missouri ex rel. Gaines v. Canada, 305 U.S. 337 (1938).

5. Sweatt v. Painter, 339 U.S. 629 (1950) and McLaurin v. Oklahoma State Regents (1950).

6. I. G. Hendricks, "Self Restraint: Concepts Perpetuating Separate But Equal Doctrine in Public Education, 1849-1954," *Journal of Law and Education,* 12 (October 1983), pp. 561-585. See especially pp. 575-581.

7. R. L. Carter, "The Right to Equal Educational Opportunity," in N. Dorsen, ed., *The Rights of Americans* (New York: Random House, 1972), pp. 6-20; and Carter, "A Reassessment of Brown v. Board," pp. 24-25.

8. Hendrick, "Self Restraint," p. 575.

9. Carter, "A Reassessment of Brown v. Board," p. 23.

10. Brown v. Board of Education (1954)

11. Brown v. Board of Education (1955).

12. R. Kluger, *Simple Justice* (New York: Alfred A. Knopf, 1976), pp. 750-751.

13. Briggs v. Elliott, 132 F. Supp. 776 (1955); see also Ibid., pp. 751-752.

14. Kluger, *Simple Justice,* pp. 726-727, 752-763.

15. Ibid., pp. 759-761.

16. W. V. Grant and T. D. Snyder, *Digest of Education Statistics 1983-84,* National Center for Education Statistics Report No. NCES-83-407/ERIC No. ED244 402 (21st ed.; Washington, D.C., NCES, 1983), p. 3; and "Private Schools Grow, Public Rolls Down," *The Birmingham News* (Alabama), December 20, 1984, p. 17A.

17. Grant and Snyder, *Digest of Education Statistics 1983-84,* p. 41.

18. Bell, ed., *Shades of Brown,* p. ix.

19. Ibid., p. 94; and V. S. Allen, "Integration and Higher Education," *Integrateducation,* 20, Nos. 3-5 (May–October 1982), pp. 65-66.

20. T. Sowell, *Black Education: Myths and Tragedies* (New York: David McKay, 1972), pp. 283-287.

21. B. M. Wilson, "Racial Segregation Trends in Birmingham, Alabama," *Southeastern Geographer,* 25 (May 1985), pp. 2-9.

22. Carter, "A Reassessment of Brown v. Board," p. 26.

23. D. P. Moynihan used the term in making a similar suggestion in 1970 that "the time may have come when the issue of race could benefit from a period of benign neglect...in which Negro progress continues and racial rhetoric fades." He was severely criticized.

24. A. O. White, "Florida's Functional Literacy Test on Trial," *Urban Education*, 19 (April 1984), p. 18; C. Ascher, "Helping Minority Students with Nontraditional Skills to Enter and Complete College," *Urban Review*, 16 (January 1984), pp. 57–58; and "Suit Against Tuscaloosa's Tough New School Standards to Be Landmark Case?" *The Birmingham News* (Alabama), October 7, 1982, p. 5F.

25. Brown v. Board of Education (1954).

26. National Association of Social Workers, *Code of Ethics* (Silver Spring, Md.: NASW, 1980), Sec. VI, p. 9.

27. Sowell, *Black Education.*

28. W. Schwartz, "Private Troubles and Public Issues: One Social Work Job or Two?" in R. W. Klenk and R. M. Ryan, eds., *The Practice of Social Work* (2nd ed.; Belmont, Calif.: Wadsworth Publishing Co., 1974); N. Goroff, "Ideology, Sociological Theories, and Public Policy," *Journal of Sociology and Social Welfare*, 1 (Fall 1973); and H. Wilensky and C. N. Lebeaux, *Industrial Society and Social Welfare* (New York: Macmillan, 1965).

29. P. Gurin and E. Epps, *Black Consciousness, Identity and Achievement* (New York: John Wiley & Sons, 1975), see especially Chap. 1 and pp. 95–105.

30. T. M. Tomlinson, "The Troubled Years: An Interpretive Analysis of Public Schooling Since 1950," *Phi Delta Kappan*, 62 (January 1981); and A. Arcuri, W. Daly, and P. Mercado, "Today's Students Want to Take Pride in Their Work," *Chronicle of Higher Education*, 25 (September 8, 1982).

31. J. P. Dolly and D. P. Page, "An Attempt to Increase Parental Involvement in Rural Schools," *Phi Delta Kappan*, 64 (March 1983), p. 512.

32. S. L. Lightfoot, "Families as Educators," in Bell, *Shades of Brown;* and P. H. Shields and D. Dupree, "Influence of Parent Practices upon the Reading Achievement of Good and Poor Readers," *Journal of Negro Education*, 52 (Fall 1983), pp. 436–445.

33. Lightfoot, "Families as Educators," p. 4.

34. Carter, "A Reassessment of Brown v. Board," p. 28.

Contributors

Mable T. Hawkins, Ph.D., is Associate Professor, School of Social Work, University of Pittsburgh, Pittsburgh, Pennsylvania. She is First Vice President of the National Association of Social Workers.

Robin H. Aronow, DSW, is School Social Worker, East Meadow School District, East Meadow, New York. She is also affiliated with Nassau County Department of Drug and Alcohol Addiction and New York State Division of Substance Abuse.

Nancy Kramer Banchy, MSW, is Assistant Director, Social Work Services, Minneapolis Public Schools, Minneapolis, Minnesota.

Don Bebee, MSW, is Assistant Professor, Social Work Program, University of Arkansas, Fayetteville.

Marilyn Sargon Brier, MSW, is Clinical Social Worker, Visiting Nurse Association of South Middlesex Hospice Program, Framingham, Massachusetts. At the time of writing, she was affiliated with Pathways for Children, Massachusetts Hospital School, Canton.

Susan H. Dawson, MA, is Professor, School of Social Work, Louisiana State University, Baton Rouge.

Harry K. Dillard, MA, is Director of Pupil Services, Winnetka Public Schools, Winnetka, Illinois.

Beverly Donenberg, MAT, is Learning Disabilities Specialist, Winnetka Public Schools, Winnetka, Illinois.

Jackolyn W. Durrett, MSW, is Assistant Professor, School of Social Work, Louisiana State University, Baton Rouge.

Carol Ethridge, BA, is a graduate student in rehabilitation counseling, University of Arkansas, Fayetteville.

Janice Furman, MSW, is School Social Worker, Fairfax County Public Schools, Fairfax, Virginia.

Antonio Gambini, MSW, is School Social Worker, Student Services Department, Toronto Board of Education, Toronto, Ontario, Canada.

Elizabeth Floyd Gerlock, MS, is Director of Agency Services, Middle Tennessee Department of Mental Health/Mental Retardation, Nashville.

Harriet Glickman, MSW, is Social Worker and In-Service Coordinator, Winnetka Public Schools, Winnetka, Illinois.

Gregory Grande, DSW, is Senior Social Worker, Student Services Department, Toronto Board of Education, Toronto, Ontario, Canada.

Valerie Gray, MSW, is Adoption Specialist, Baton Rouge Regional Office of Human Development, Division of Children, Youth and Family Services, Department of Health and Human Resources, Baton Rouge, Louisiana.

Betty Guhman, MSW, is Assistant Professor, Social Work Program, University of Arkansas, Fayetteville.

Renee Shai Levine, DSW, is Assistant Professor, School of Social Work, University of Pennsylvania, Philadelphia.

Debra M. Meckley, MSW, is Social Worker, Catholic Social Services, Lancaster, Pennsylvania

Mary Constance Patterson, MSW, is Clinical and School Social Worker, Parkland Psychiatric Hospital, Baton Rouge, Louisiana.

Judith Pratt, MSW, is School Social Worker, Fairfax County Public Schools, Fairfax, Virginia.

Marie Rothschild, MSW, was formerly Social Work Supervisor, Herbert G. Birch School for Exceptional Children, Springfield Gardens, New York, and is currently in private practice in psychotherapy, Rockville Centre, New York.

Donna S. Swall, MSW, is School Social Worker, Lawrence Unified School District 497, and is Executive Director of Families Together, Inc., Lawrence, Kansas.

Forrest L. Swall, MSSW, is Director of the Baccalaureate Program, School of Social Welfare, University of Kansas, Lawrence.

Gayle Twilbeck Wykle, Ph.D., is Associate Professor, Department of Social Work, University of Alabama at Birmingham.